DON'T CHASE HAPPINESS!
36 RULES TO A FULFILLING LIFE, IN THE MODERN WORLD

DON'T CHASE HAPPINESS!

36 RULES TO A FULFILLING LIFE, IN THE MODERN WORLD

JOSHUA EDELSTEIN

If you would like more information on how to retain
consulting services or mentorship, whether professional or
personal, please contact:
thestrategicperspective@gmail.com
Or visit:
www.thestrategicperspective.com

TO THOSE HERE AND GONE, WHO HAVE SHAPED MY UNDERSTANDING OF THE WORLD.

CONTENTS

PREFACE:

Are you your own biggest roadblock to personal fulfillment? If I told you the phrase, "Personal fulfillment" was an oxymoron, would you believe me? In a, "Focus on what makes you happy!", "If it feels good, do it!", "Me!" based culture, ironically pushed by the self-improvement movement of the 1970s and 1980s, you probably wouldn't.

Allow me to explain. Human beings are social creatures and while your goal should be to live a more fulfilling life, you need more than just yourself and the pursuit of personal happiness to feel truly fulfilled. Therefore, to be personally happy, personally fulfilled and personally satisfied, the first thing you need to do is drop the word "Personal" from your vocabulary. At the very least, lower its importance.

In this book, I will dismantle some of the lessons taught by self-help gurus of the past, who spawned the, "Me! Culture" to begin with. Within these pages, I will teach you how to create the kind of fulfilling life that you have always wanted. A life that not only benefits you but also your friends, your family, and society.

I have taken care to write this book in a non-religious way, for I myself do not subscribe to any one religion. With that being said, I hold great respect to your own personal religious beliefs and have studied many of them. A few of these rules may even resemble lessons taught by some. I may point out similarities or historical figures from time to time but will never take it further than that. Whatever your beliefs or non-beliefs may be, in organized religion, I urge you to have an open mind.

The source doesn't make a specific lesson or piece of advice, any more or any less true. For example, you don't have to be Christian or religious at all to understand, "You should not commit murder" as a good, general rule to live your life by.

The year is 2019 and the United States is more politically polarized than at any time since The Civil War. For this reason, I have done my best to write this book in a completely apolitical way. I think most people will agree with that sentiment unless you are heavily partisan to one side or another. If that is the case, no matter what "side you're on", you may disagree with me on certain points and agree with me on others.

The 36 rules that I have laid out will benefit everyone in our society and will hopefully play some role in bringing us all back together again. This may be too lofty a goal, however, there is nothing in any rule laid out that is meant to be offensive to anyone, of any faith, ethnicity, gender, political affiliation or sexual orientation. It is meant to be a middle ground of rules we should all try to follow. The more people that follow them, the more fulfilled we will be, collectively and individually.

There may be some hard truths when speaking of challenges, shortcuts, and emotions. Question what you read and ask yourself honestly, "Does this make sense to me?" Always question everything you read, hear or see but do not outright dismiss or agree with anything due to preconceived notions. The goal is to learn as much as you can and preconceived notions will always be your biggest barrier to growth.

You may have first heard the term, "Me generation" to describe Baby Boomers. They were the first generation, to put more emphasis on the self than the community and traditional family values. People were finally comfortable enough, as a society, to start actively seeking out personal happiness and individualism as a concept. They are the generation that grew self-improvement into the multi-billion-dollar industry that it is today. They also invented the TV dinner. Before that, it was virtually unheard of to have a family meal not seated around the kitchen table together. Today, the opposite holds true.

I don't mean to bash on you if you are a Baby Boomer. You can benefit from this book just as much as anyone else. With that being said, this book was written with a slightly different tone, for a slightly different audience. There is not as much material available for later Generation X'ers and younger, to inspire growth and overcome the challenges presented by the modern world.

The quest for personal happiness that started with Baby Boomers has now crossed over into multiple generations. With each new generation, this focus on the self over others has grown stronger and stronger. This, in turn, has made community and family, along with longstanding traditions, weaker and less relevant. I like to use the term,

"Me! Culture" to describe our current situation and it the biggest enemy to fulfillment. Self-indulgence, self-importance and self-aggrandizing are now accepted as normal, even celebrated parts of life.

This, "Me! culture" is cancer. It has mutated the cells of our society, slowly destroying it from the inside out. This societal cancer plays a large role in the rapid uptick of mental health issues, rising prescription / recreational drug use and the lowering of happiness trends reported in statistic after statistic.

Despite all the promising developments of the past century, to make our lives better, we have forgotten or in many cases, were never taught the rules to live a life of fulfillment. Living a fulfilling life is the treatment to this cancer. If enough people start living by the 36 rules to fulfillment, we can cure this societal cancer for good, before it becomes too late.

To illustrate, let me start with a dare. I dare you to open your social media platform of choice and try to find a post or image, from one of your "friends", glamorizing themselves or their lifestyle. My bet is that it will take you less than 10 seconds.

Look at your own profile now. Can you spot a message or picture that you posted, to make yourself look better, happier, more enlightened or having more fun than actual reality, to gain social capital or to make someone else feel jealous?

It's become such a normal way of life, I'm willing to bet you can find several. Someone living a truly fulfilling life would be far too busy enjoying themselves to waste any time or soil their experience with this kind of behavior.

Now open your web browser and click on Yahoo, Salon, Slate or really any website that posts news articles and opinion pieces. Once there, you will immediately see links and statements full of hate, negativity, personal attacks and bullying of people you don't personally know, really don't care about and in most cases, will never affect your physical day to day life.

Within the comment sections of the above articles, you are bound to find endless hours of people arguing about anything and everything.

Now a healthy debate is one thing and can be very entertaining, if not fulfilling. My concern is the level of vitriol expressed by people in these threads. Horrible insults are thrown around without a care, even death is wished upon people who simply do not agree with them.

Acting in this way would never cross the mind of someone living a fulfilling life. It is, however, one more symptom of this cancer, leading to the downfall of our society.

Yet, this book is not a condemnation of technology, our modern lifestyle or even some of the vices we have developed. Modern technology and the continued development of the world will benefit us greatly.

Enjoying a glass of wine or a beer in the company of friends and family can do wonders in creating the fulfillment that you seek. Mind you, it's not the wine or beer but the company and conversation that is creating the actual fulfillment.

At the beginning of this book, modern challenges and shortcuts to happiness are highlighted, only out of necessity. Just as a General must understand their enemy and the challenges they present, we must also understand our challenges and the reasoning behind them, before we can attempt to make any lasting change.

For this reason, I urge you to read this book all the way through, at least once. In one section, I will describe the eight, primary human emotions. Learning about why we feel the way we do brings incite, incite upon why we sometimes act the way we do.

I have placed the 36 rules to a fulfilling life near the last section of this book, prior to the conclusion. Being armed with the information learned before will help you understand the importance of each rule. It will also help give you the strength needed to follow them. They will not always be easy. Nothing worth anything ever is.

Bookmark certain rules that you want to go back to, or that you are having trouble with. If there are specific rules that you want to focus on at any given time, write them on notes to remind yourself throughout the day. Use technology to your advantage and set reminders on your phone.

I will promise you in advance, reading this book will not make you happy all the time. Even if you live by every rule laid out, all 36 like gospel, you will not be happy all the time. Anyone who tells you they can make your life happy all the time by going to their seminar, taking this pill or that pill, or my personal favorite, "Just thinking in a positive way" is being disingenuous at best.

Happiness is an emotion and an emotion, by definition, is a fluid and fleeting state of being. If you read this book and live by the tried and true rules I have laid out, rules that have been tested for generations, you will live a much more fulfilled life. Fulfillment should always be your goal. It is a much deeper state of being than happiness or any other emotion. Think of fulfillment as your foundation.

Must you live by all 36 rules to have a more fulfilling life? No! Absolutely not. However, the more rules that you follow, the more fulfilling your life will be, the more frequent your happy times will be, the richer and more rewarding your experiences will be and the stronger your foundation will be when the forces of life try and shake you.

Life can be a bitch or a garden of roses, sometimes simultaneously. If your foundation is strong, it will not crumble. No matter what is thrown at it.

This book is not a shortcut. It is not a secret or a tool made for manipulation. This is a book of rules, of non-religious doctrine, a book of guidelines. This is a book that when followed and integrated into your life, will bring success and prosperity in all its forms.

The information contained within may not always feel new, shocking or profound. That was not my goal. This is not a social experiment with a ton of new, unverified theory.

My purpose was to arrange this timeless information together, in a way that makes sense to you. To offer a new perspective. One that leads you to see how many of the things that create fulfillment are interconnected. There are 36 rules to fulfillment but many times, when you follow one as it is intended, you will also be following several them at the same time.

I would like to offer you one warning: Do not read this book with the intention of manipulating others. Following the basic outline of these rules, with the wrong intentions, may still bring you social and financial prosperity.

Fortunately, even if you start following these rules for the wrong reasons, it is likely that your outlook will change, especially as you witness the positive results of your actions. You will start to fill a void within your heart. A void that you may have not previously recognized. Use this moment of clarity to understand that fulfillment is possible, even for you.

I wrote down the outline and 36 rules for a very personal reason. To act as a kind of insurance policy. If something should ever happen to me, I can still give my son guidance throughout his life.

To try and do more good than harm, I have turned this outline into a book. This book itself was written with a much larger audience in mind and with a solitary purpose: To help bring actual fulfillment into the lives of real people, in an ever-increasing, ever unfulfilling, modern, cyber-based world.

I hope you enjoy reading this book as much as I have enjoyed writing it.

SECTION 1: 6 CHALLENGES TO FULFILLMENT IN THE MODERN WORLD

While there are more than six challenges to fulfillment, I would like to highlight six that previous generations have not had to deal with to our current extent. These six challenges are so prevalent, even accepted, that some of you may want to scoff and call me, "Out of date!"

I am on the cusp of Generation X and The Millennials, depending upon which article you read. Most have me pegged right at the beginning of The Millennial Generation.

I can remember a time before technology was prevalent or the internet even existed. When children still played outside until the streetlights came on and we had to use our imaginations more than screens for entertainment. Video games were primitive and fun but not so fun that you wouldn't rather be outside, running around with friends.

I watched as technology advanced with excitement and enthusiasm. I still do for that matter. I was also a witness to the rise of these six challenges, even a participant in some. This gives me a unique perspective that someone much older or younger, might not have.

Three have been bad from the start and time has only made them worse. The other three still have the potential to cause more good than harm, depending upon how they are used.

Without further ado, here are the six challenges to fulfillment in the modern world:

CHALLENGE 1 - THE "ME! CULTURE":

I touched upon this during the preface because it is probably the biggest challenge to overcome on the path to fulfillment, both individually and societally. You will see this, "Me! Culture" emerge as a pattern, in some of the other challenges to fulfillment.

First let me be clear that when talking about, "Me! Culture" I am not talking about suppressing individualism in all forms and certainly not self-expression.

People need to be free to be themselves and live their own truth. If their truth doesn't directly infringe on the life or protected beliefs of anyone else, this is a major part of living a fulfilling life. Hiding who you are from yourself or anyone else goes against the freedom we have been granted and is flat out deceptive.

At the same time, we must be careful not to go too far. The same rights that allow you to live the life you want also protect the lives of others who choose to live differently.

We cannot shut down or silence the voices of those we do not agree with, in the name of political correctness. (Those of you on the far left may disagree with me on this last sentence. Don't worry, the far right may disagree with me soon as well - and back and forth throughout.) An open and respectful dialog is the only solution if we want to live in a civilized society.

In the past, we have been bound by the strict rules of government or religion to conform. If you veered even the slightest from what was considered normal, this lead to ostracization, oppression and a whole bunch of other evil stuff that is the antithesis of fulfillment.

However, not everything is good and not everything is evil. Many of those societal rules, at least the basis behind them, were positive and led to the formation of civilization.

To find happiness in the modern world, in some regard, we've thrown the baby out with the bathwater. One rule that helped keep us together and connected was placing a higher emphasis on serving others over ourselves and working as a team towards a common goal. Society over self. We needed to do this for basic survival in the old, rough and tumble world of the past. You needed to know you could count on your neighbors for help if you were in need, just as your neighbors knew they could count on you. This created a sense of community and connected us all together in a bond.

Today, it seems the opposite viewpoint is taken. Everyone is concerned with how many "likes" THEY receive on a social media post, what is on THEIR wish lists, what they can't wait to buy THEMSELVES on Black Friday (Traditionally started to buy family members Christmas gifts after seeing them on Thanksgiving, after talking and finding out things they might like).

You get the idea. People now spend more money "self-gifting" during Black Friday than on gifts for family members and friends.

The focus on trying to make yourself happy is ironically one of the biggest roadblocks to actual, lasting happiness. It's also the reason the typical buyer of self-improvement books will buy at least one new book on self-help every year and a half or so.

Breaking this habit, the "Me! Culture" is a major trend in the 36 rules to fulfillment and as I already mentioned, one of the most important.

CHALLENGE 2 - SOCIAL MEDIA:

The idea behind social media is a wonderful thing: A tool to be used in aiding connection and contact with those close to you. This tool is especially useful in helping to keep in touch with close friends and family members separated by long, physical distances.

How can this possibly be a challenge to fulfillment? If anything, shouldn't a tool so useful in human connection, a pillar of life fulfillment only be good? Of course, you already know the answer and if life were that simple, I wouldn't be writing this book.

One basic challenge social media presents is how much time it takes out of our day. How many hours a day do you spend scrolling through social media feeds on your phone or computer?

As of right now, Americans spend an average of nearly 2.5 hours per day interacting on social media. That is 2.5 hours out of every waking moment they could be present, having face to face conversations, playing with their children, working to advance their careers, a side business or any other number of things. This is just the average. Keep in mind there are many people that spend way more time than this.

Social media also takes us out of the moment. Aside from the direct time spent looking at your screen, how much time have you spent trying to get that perfect selfie during a truly special time or place? A moment that may never happen to you again. Do you do this to show everyone how cool/cultured/enlightened/fun/happy you are? Just to make yourself feel socially validated? Or worse, to compete with all your other online, "Friends" that do the same thing?

Part of that goes back to the, "Me! Culture. " Even if those weren't your intentions, it's still taking you out of a special moment that you are now, not fully appreciating.

Pictures are a great tool of reflection, bringing you back to happy or important times in your life. Please don't think I'm trashing them completely. There is a limit though.

Do you really need 10 photos of a Pina colada, sitting on a table, overlooking a Caribbean sunset? Feel the warm sea breeze, participate in a conversation with the people you are with and enjoy the damn sunset already!

I can go on and on about the pitfalls of social media, including how it's increasingly cited as a main factor in divorce. It may be hard to believe but there is something even more nefarious that must be addressed about social media.

Social media is the root cause of cyberbullying, especially in adolescents and teenagers. As if growing up wasn't hard enough, especially for an awkward child getting bullied at school. At least there used to be a break in communication between kids. A timeout for bullies to forget about their targets. (Ironically and sadly, this is when bullies are bullied themselves by those that are older and should be caring for them.) A timeout for the victim to recuperate. A timeout for people to forget about the embarrassing thing that happened to them.

Now, that embarrassing thing lives online forever, for the whole world to see and pass judgment on. Especially if caught on camera by someone...And everyone has a camera at the ready...All the time!

These are a few of the many reasons why social media poses a huge risk to society in general. There are also studies and testimony, from top social media executives, warning how social media has been engineered to be as physically and psychologically addictive as possible. To keep you coming back for more and more screen time, more dopamine hits, more "likes" and more ad dollars.

Please use caution if you choose to use social media. Depending upon how it is used, social media can be a dangerous deterrent to a fulfilling life. Will time be cruel to social media, in the history books of tomorrow? If we keep traveling the same path, then yes.

It doesn't have to be. If society changes for the better, how social media is used will as well.

CHALLENGE 3 - VIDEO GAMES:

I won't dive too deep into this because modern video games pose a lot of the same risks of social media. This is partially because social media is a huge component built into many of the most popular video games.

There are two unique threats video games pose to a real, fulfilling life. The first is that they create a fake, cyber life in an alternate reality. You can be anything you want to be in this alternate reality and that is very addicting. It literally pulls you out of your real life, like a dream you can control. Dreams can be wonderful but do you really want to spend your whole life sleeping?

Likewise, it can be healthy to escape reality from time to time with video games but only when done so in moderation. Otherwise, it becomes an addiction, much like an alcoholic escaping their real lives inside of a bottle.

Living in this alternate, cyber reality, no matter how great it may seem, is no substitution for creating a fulfilling life, based in actual reality - the real world.

The other risk associated with video games is that for the most part, they keep you sedentary. To live a fulfilling life, one needs to stay active and get out into nature as often as possible. You don't have to be the perfect picture of physical health to have a fulfilling life. I will repeat this over and over.

Aside from the physical exercise, there is also something very inspiring, refreshing and therapeutic with breathing in the fresh air, being outdoors and feeling the sunshine (Vitamin D) upon your skin.

CHALLENGE 4 - TECHNOLOGY:

Technology, in general, can be as big of a challenge to a fulfilling life as it can be an aid to a fulfilling life. There are so many different types of technology in so many industries that I won't even begin to make an argument one way or another. It is just something to be mindful of and realistically, all about how you use it.

CHALLENGE 5 - THE BREAKDOWN OF THE FAMILY UNIT:

This can be a politically charged topic, depending upon how you are looking at it and what you consider a family unit. My definition for this purpose is two loving parents, doing their best to spend time with, teach values/ethics to and raise their children into educated, responsible, contributing members of society.

Depending upon the charts you are reading, divorce rates appear to hit the highest rates between the mid-1970s to the mid-1980s. I think there are many reasons for this and can't help associate at least some of it with the rise of the, "Me! Culture" and quest for the Moby Dick of personal happiness.

Correlation certainly doesn't equal causation but thinking, "Me" instead of, "We" is very detrimental to any relationship.

Every relationship starts with feelings of infatuation and potentially an emotional, chemical reaction we like to call, "Falling in love".

However, problems always arise. There are different problems in every relationship. Learning how to work through these problems and grow a commitment to each other is always more fulfilling than jumping from relationship to relationship.

Obviously, in cases of abuse, this is different but most couple's differences can be worked out if the desire to do so is there. This is a decision that only you and your partner can make together. Be sure to marry the right person for you!

Online dating has presented a new challenge. It is so easy to meet new people now, even for those that are shy. Not everyone will be a match and that is expected. If you are not a match, thank them for their time and move on.

The problems start after that first connection is made. Emotions start to develop, we get a little more comfortable and, "Gasp!" become human. It's so easy to jump from relationship to relationship, chasing that infatuation stage when everyone is on their best behavior and we all seem perfect.

This pattern is very similar to a drug abuser with one major difference. The drug user's best experience is typically the first. No matter how many times they use, trying to recreate that feeling is impossible, try as they might.

With relationships, it is very easy to recreate that feeling. All you need to do is dump the person you're with once the infatuation starts to mature into something deeper and the initial chemicals wear off.

With the deepening of a relationship, the chemical response that created the feelings of, 'In love" starts to mature into emotions built on a logical foundation where "True love" can develop. Trust in each other has been established and a certain level of comfort is achieved. Do not confuse comfort with boredom as it is easy to ruin a good thing for the wrong reasons.

Likewise, these new feelings may not be comfortable for those with trust issues (More on this later) as the more you open up, the more vulnerable you become. If you can't get past these feelings or to the contrary, if you are in constant search of that initial chemical infatuation, you will never feel truly fulfilled within any relationship.

Luckily, even with these challenges, divorce rates are heading downward, which is a very positive trend and a sign that people are taking marriage and commitment more seriously.

The more concerning statistic is the rise in out of wedlock birth rates around the world. They are growing in extreme rates which leads to more and more children growing up without the love and support of two parents.

I am a parent myself, to one child that I share with my wife. We both work full-time jobs but do everything we can to provide our son with the best life possible. This includes spending as much quality time together as we can.

He is lucky and will most likely grow up with advantages that many other children will not. Even still, being a modern dad in a two-parent household is incredibly challenging. With only one child! We are also fortunate enough to have my Mom living nearby and she is more than willing to help... a lot!

Notwithstanding my anecdotal experience as a father in a two-parent household, there are a slew of statistics citing the advantages of having two active parents. Children growing up in two-parent households behave better in school, score higher on tests and are far less likely to end up in gangs and the criminal justice system.

Now there are plenty of single parents that do an excellent job of raising exceptional children. Those parents have my full admiration as I can only imagine the energy, patience, and determination that takes. As unfortunate as it may be, those parents are a statistical minority, by far.

Most of us end up somewhere in the middle when it comes to our families. We all have problems.

None of our parents were perfect because none of their parents were perfect. I think it's safe to say, none of us are perfect either.

We can all benefit from a little more fulfillment in our lives. That is why it is never too early or never too late to learn and live by the 36 rules to a fulfilling life.

CHALLENGE 6 - HYPERSENSITIVITY:

In the west, we have gone soft as a society. This is at least partially accountable to the breakdown in the family unit. To create the right balance of strength and empathy, while growing up, children need the right balance of masculine and feminine energy.

Notice I say masculine and feminine energy, not necessarily male and female parents. I say this because, in many same-sex relationships, one partner tends to naturally take on the more masculine role and the other, the more feminine role (The alpha and beta).

It is harder to provide that in a one parent household. Most single-parent households are led by a single mother (Again, speaking only to the majority here), who's natural character tends to be more feminine and empathizing.

For them, it becomes much more difficult to instill the toughness and discipline needed to thrive in the modern world, especially for boys.

If you cannot provide a child with the right balance of love and discipline, logic and emotion, this creates a teenager that is at risk and ripe for the manipulation of their moral character.

"Sticks and stones may break my bones but words can never hurt me" used to be the verbal answer and frame of mind when you were picked on by a bully. It seems that we have become so weak as a society, that statement no longer holds true.

When asked if a verbal assault, (By the way, there is legally no such thing) deserves a physically violent response, many people say, "Yes."

This is a hypersensitive, emotional reaction. Words can only hurt if you let them. A punch in the face even hurts professional fighters.

"No one can make you feel inferior without your consent"–Eleanor Roosevelt

In a world where we are so hypersensitive that, "Micro-aggression" and "Dog whistle" are terms commonly used in pop-culture, to describe potentially offensive words or actions, is a clear indication of severe unfulfillment in people's lives. At this point, you are actively seeking out the offense (Where there is most often, no ill intention.).

People whose lives are legitimately fulfilled would never recognize a "Micro-aggression" or "Dog whistle". These types of, "Insults" have as much potential to be innocent words or phrases made in normal conversation as they do hidden, metaphoric insults. Remember, "Sometimes a cigar is just a cigar." – Sigmund Freud.

In the mind of someone truly fulfilled and of strong character, they are never the victim of so-called, "Verbal attacks."

They may recognize the anger or ignorance in the voice or the words of another person, but the words will not stick. The truly fulfilled person will feel empathy for the other person. They will also feel sympathy for their ignorance and let the words roll off their backs, like beads of water off a freshly waxed car.

Even in two-parent households, there is a trend emerging to suppress the balance of feminine and masculine energy. This trend has been titled, "Toxic masculinity" which is a dead giveaway to its true purpose.

There is an equal amount of toxic behavior and healthy behavior on both the masculine and feminine sides of one's character. They are simply different and will manifest themselves in different ways.

If the intention was to simply stop people from behaving badly, from behaving toxically, it would just be labeled, "Toxic behavior" while dropping the word masculinity. As mentioned above, suppressing one's masculinity will not help make anyone, let alone society, fulfilled. There must be a balance of traits in everyone and balance is never achieved by simply removing one part of a complex equation.

Toxic behavior in general is partially due to removing or lessening the importance of a typically feminine characteristic from our society.

That characteristic is compassion/empathy for other people. Once again, this can be traced back to the, "Me! Culture" our society has embraced. Instead of trying to suppress nature and biology, we should be trying to place greater emphasis on certain positive traits within us all.

We haven't completely dropped compassion/empathy from society. If we had, that would make us all literal sociopaths. Instead, we have let it degrade into a tweet or other online statement of disingenuous outrage, in defense of whatever the popular, "Marginalized group" of the day is.

Even though this tweet does nothing but create more division and only takes a few seconds, it tricks the brain into thinking they are being compassionate, empathetic to one's plight and making a positive contribution to society. Then, most of the time, we go about our day as if nothing happened. That is how you know our response to the outrageous statement was disingenuous.

In other words, we have become a society that wants to do the least amount of work for the most feel-good hormones. A quick happiness fix to satisfy a basic human need. Another term for this is, "Lazy".

The problem is, much like a shot of your favorite spirit or hit of your drug of choice, that feeling doesn't last. Not only does it not last, it does nothing to provide you with real, lasting fulfillment.

It is good to be passionate about helping others. Providing genuine help to those in need. I think most people agree with this statement no matter where you fall on the political spectrum.

The solution is where things get tricky. Some feel that we should give to everyone down on their luck, with their hand out. Some feel that luck is created and it is better to teach a man to fish, rather than give him one. Some think we should help the world while others think we should help, "Our own" first.

I feel that every situation should be treated differently, knowing sometimes, the best help you can give someone is no help at all. I do know you should be kind to others and get involved with your community to make a positive impact, not for social capital. Those things always lead to greater fulfillment.

On a positive note, since that trait is still living inside most of us, we can relearn how to manifest it into something truly helpful. Something that does genuine, actual good. There are many people that still do this.

There are plenty of organizations whose sole purpose is to do good. I'm not endorsing either organization but take "Habitat for Humanity" or "Doctors without Borders" as good examples of this. Both organizations lift people up, without putting anyone else down.

In addition to these organizations, we must bring this kind of compassion/empathy back into our society, on a micro, day to day level throughout the whole year. We tend to see this kind of action around the month of December. That is part of what makes the holidays feel so magical and special.

If we can take this step: helping others in real, tangible ways, throughout the entire year, it will do a great deal towards making us all feel more fulfilled.

SECTION 2: UNDERSTANDIND THE 8 PRIMARY HUMAN EMOTIONS

There are 8 primary human emotions, as written by Dr. Robert Plutchik, a Psychologist who received his Ph.D. from Columbia University and was Professor Emeritus at the Albert Einstein College of Medicine: Fear, Anger, Sadness, Joy, Disgust, Trust, Anticipation and Surprise.

As you will note, four of these emotions can be clearly seen as negative, two are positive and two can go either way. Out of all the possible, primary emotions, you can feel, only two of them are strictly positive. This is what makes life so challenging but also what makes life so interesting. It is also what makes chasing happiness futile.

Is it possible to master all your emotions, use them to your betterment and for the betterment of society? To reach enlightenment? I don't know for sure, though I urge you to try.

I look at it like mastering the game of golf. If it is possible, it will probably take a lifetime of practice. Some days you will play a nearly perfect game and some days you won't be able to stay out of the rough, or the sand trap, or the water hazard. Also, like golf, the more you practice, the more of those good games you will play.

A good strategy is to recognize your most damaging emotions. Emotions that you have the hardest time controlling. Work on these first. Eat the whale one bite at a time and it won't feel so overwhelming.

You can use different words to create emotions with greater or lesser intensity. You may also combine emotions to create different feelings, this is called, "The Emotional Wheel" and is used much like colors on a color wheel. When looked upon this way, there are approximately 34,000 different emotions a human can feel. Like the color wheel, containing 3 primary colors, your typical Pantone book contains over 1800 different solid colors.

You may notice that "Love" is not listed as a primary emotion. This is because Dr. Plutchik categorized love as a combination of joy and trust. This is actually very important to understand and will be gone into with greater depth shortly.

EMOTION 1 - FEAR:

As defined by Merriam-Webster, fear is an unpleasant often strong emotion caused by anticipation or awareness of danger.

Fear can be mild or cripplingly debilitating. It can come often or be felt rarely. It can be based on real danger and is an important mechanism of survival when acted upon appropriately.

That is the purpose of this primary emotion. It can also be based on imaginative or ill-conceived danger. When felt irrationally, fear is unhealthy and a major barrier to a fulfilling life.

We all have a fight or flight response built into us. Without getting too physiological, when facing danger, whether real or imagined, the body's autonomic nervous system (ANS), specifically the sympathetic nervous system is activated by a release of adrenaline, noradrenaline, and catecholamines by stimulation of the adrenal glands.

This immediately gives the body a sudden burst of energy. The kind of energy needed to either fight to the death or run for your life. While still, an important function in modern society, having this kind of strong hormone release is very stressful on the body and the mind.

Irrational fear is common in all of us from time to time. Many of us like to be scared. That's why horror movies, psychological thrillers, and haunted attractions are so popular.

If the fear is irrational, undesirable and is something you recognize as such, it can be fought. We must do all we can to overcome irrational fear because you can fight through it and win. Never let fear stop you from doing what you want, or asking for what you need.

Certain paranoid, mental health conditions are based on the strength of this primary emotion. Those worst afflicted will constantly look everywhere for all signs of danger.

Even though the modern world is much safer than most of history, the danger is getting easier and easier to find.

All you must do is look online at the myriad of conspiracy theorists. They will feed your irrational fears with videos, articles, pictures and all kinds of "proof" something or someone is out to get you.

A lot of these people have legitimate, paranoid psychological conditions and don't even know it. It becomes difficult to see and recognize fear as irrational if it's being validated by hundreds, if not thousands of other people.

When these feelings are felt often, due to irrational thoughts, phobias or social situations, this is a major impairment to a fulfilling life. Many people, once they recognize their fear is due to internal vs external factors will find regular, cognitive behavioral therapy useful.

The hardest part, even before the internet is recognizing when you have a legitimate, paranoid condition based on internal factors.

I mean no disrespect but there is a joke that illustrates this, "Real crazy doesn't understand that they are crazy."

The 36 rules to live by will most certainly help. When combined with professional therapy you can bring about a real, life-changing experience.

EMOTION 2 - ANGER:

Anger is defined as a strong feeling of displeasure and usually of antagonism. It can be felt as low as a slight irritation or as high as a furious, uncontrollable rage.

In any event, your body undergoes a physiological response like fear with a release of adrenaline and noradrenaline, blood pressure rises along with heart rate, breathing rate and/or depth can also increase, along with diaphoresis (sweating). Even if you do a good job of hiding the outward signs, your body is still dealing with the physical symptoms of this emotion.

Anger, while not necessarily an emotion conducive to fulfillment, can and should be expressed in a healthy way. In an ideal world, one would be able to replace anger with forgiveness, love, and empathy.

Even though we live in a world far from ideal, it is still a worthy goal to strive towards on your path to fulfillment.

As social creatures living amongst each other, we are bound to have conflict from time to time and realistically, each conflict has the potential to stimulate the emotion of anger in one or more involved parties.

The trick in most cases is to communicate what has stimulated that anger early and respectfully.

If you hold onto the anger and are unable to release it yourself, it only grows. As it grows you will either let it out in an unhealthy way, an over-reactive way or, it will fester inside, punishing only yourself for the action of another. Be respectful during conflicts with others!

There is a wonderful Buddhist quote regarding anger that aptly describes this emotion, "Anger is like holding onto a hot coal with the intent of throwing it at someone else; you are the one who gets burned."

EMOTION 3 - SADNESS:

Sadness is an emotion that almost needs no definition as we have all experienced it more often than we would have liked. The literal definition is, "Affected with or expressive of grief or unhappiness".

Sadness is the antithesis of happiness. If there were no sadness in the world, we would not know the emotion of joy and happiness.

Just as you could not tell the dark without light, you could not tell the sweet without the sour. Life would just be one long season of, "Blah".

So as much as the emotion of sadness hurts during the moment, how it can sometimes cause real, physical pain, it is a necessary part of living a full life.

Sadness helps you grow by teaching you to appreciate the good times and to appreciate the people in your life while they are still in it. Sadness is also an excellent indicator of certain aspects in your life that need focusing on during your path to fulfillment.

Those places that feel unsatisfied, that give you sadness should be looked upon internally with realistic, self-critique and changed with outward action.

When you start implementing the 36 rules to a fulfilling life, start with the rules that impact those places first. This is a guide to a better, more fulfilling life and does not have to be followed like a 12-step program.

To erase the sadness completely means to erase the love, happiness and everything that makes life worth living. If you are feeling sad, you always have the potential to feel happy again, no matter how hard it might be to believe while in the midst.

For these reasons, you will never be able to erase the sadness from your life, especially if it is a life that is fulfilling. Just know that while you are still breathing, it can always get better and it can always get worse and that is a good thing.

This book is not a silver bullet, you may hear me say this many times. There are certain clinical, chemical or even situational reasons for prolonged sadness.

While I can promise you that following the 36 rules will lead you to a better, more fulfilling life, it should not be substituted for professional, psychological care from a licensed clinician.

You should follow the 36 rules and tell your Therapist, Psychologist or Psychiatrist that you are doing so. This will give them the ability to track your progress in an objective way, over a period and give personal feedback.

EMOTION 4 - JOY:

Much like the emotion of sadness, the emotion of joy needs little introduction: A feeling of great pleasure and happiness. This seems to be the emotional state that most people are seeking to be in, most of the time.

Seeking happiness, however, is kind of like looking for the end of a rainbow: The harder you look for it, the harder it is to find. Then, when you do find it, it moves somewhere else.

There are literally hundreds of thousands of books and articles centered around finding happiness. Although it's easy to see why, as when you find it, the feeling is almost inexplicably good. The pleasure is addicting both emotionally and chemically.

There are four primary chemicals within the brain that, when stimulated, contribute to experiencing joy. They are dopamine, serotonin, oxytocin and endorphins. They are each responsible for different things and different feelings. Depending upon what you are doing, the reasoning behind the stimulation, certain chemicals are stimulated more than others.

I will give you a basic understanding of how each of these chemicals work. There is much more, in-depth information available, in just about any medium you prefer if you have an interest in exploring this further.

Think of endorphins as the rush a runner feels, giving them the strength to push through that last leg of a marathon.

When you hold your new baby for the very first time, that indescribable bond is due to a flood of oxytocin running through your body.

When an addict is searching for a fix, the excitement they experience just before inserting that needle or snorting a line is due to a dopamine release, in anticipation of how the drug will make them feel.

Serotonin is the chemical responsible for the feel-good sensation associated with happiness. Hence the pharmaceuticals centered on maintaining the right balance of it (Think SSRIs like Prozac, Zoloft, Lexapro as examples). Just the right amount and you feel contentment. A little more makes you happy and even more makes you elated. When serotonin levels are too low, this can lead to a state of depression, apathy, anger, fear, mistrust, disgust... Basically, you feel very negative and unfulfilled.

When people take the party drug, "MDMA" aka "Ecstasy", it floods their brains with serotonin levels massively higher than normal.

That is why they report feeling so happy, open, talkative and physically good as their neurons fire at incredible levels.

As I mentioned before, you can't have the good without the bad so when the drug wears off, their serotonin levels fall, generally much lower than before taking it. When this happens, the body and mind fall into an emotionally and physically depressive state, especially because the change was so drastic.

This leads to the dreaded ecstasy hangover users loath so much. Even worse, studies show that chronic use of the drug often leads to permanently lower levels of natural serotonin production.

Even scarier, chronic use is not defined. It could potentially take only one or two uses to permanently increase your risk of depression or other related psychological disorders.

Obviously, there are plenty of quick fixes to boost serotonin levels and all the other happiness chemicals. It's certainly not just done with drugs.

Whole industries are centered around the quick fix to happiness. Most of the marketing you see, for just about any product, is about creating the right mixture of those four happiness chemicals in your brain, needed to make you want to buy the item they are selling.

There are also advertising strategies focused on targeting your other emotions, even negative ones, but that's a whole different book entirely.

The main problem with the quick fix to happiness, besides potentially risking your life, is that they are also quick to subside. They don't last. Yet while all of this is true, a quick fix is not necessarily always a bad thing, when used in moderation.

Sometimes you just don't have the time or ability to go to the store, buy a bunch of healthful ingredients and cook a nutritious meal. Sometimes you're driving on a road trip or working late and are really hungry. A quick stop at a fast food joint or call for takeout will satisfy that same urge of hunger for the moment. Will it make your body feel good? Momentarily, yes. It will give you the same immediate serotonin rush as any other decent tasting meal. (FYI: Serotonin is created in the digestive system and being, "Hangry" is a real, potential outcome of this.)

This same statement may not be the case one hour later as your body struggles to extract it's needed nutrients from a meal high in saturated fats, sodium, sugar and extra calories. We'll talk more about different quick fixes, vices, and shortcuts to happiness later.

The point is that sometimes your only realistic options may be between bad and worse. In those situations, always try and pick the least harmful one that you can. Moderation is the key and sometimes, realistically, that bacon burger is more fulfilling than the salmon salad.

Joy is only one emotion within the human experience. Even naturally occurring happiness does not last forever. Naturally occurring happiness is; however, the most fulfilling and natural fulfillment often leads to feelings of happiness.

It's a very positive cycle and the greatest benefit of my 36 rules to live by. So, remember, don't chase happiness, chase fulfillment. A fulfilling life will have many happy times. Do not forget fond memories from your past and reminisce upon them often.

EMOTION 5 - DISGUST:

Merriam-Webster has two entries for the word disgust. I will choose the second entry as it contains the two definitions I feel best describes this emotion:

To provoke to loathing, repugnance, or aversion: be offensive to.

To cause (one) to lose interest or intention.

The funny thing about the emotion of disgust is that while it is classified as a primary emotion, it is not one that comes naturally to us.

Disgust must be taught, either through personal experience or shared knowledge from a trusted figure.

Disgust is an emotion that was derived to save us from things that can harm or kill us, much like fear. If you watch someone's hand disintegrate in a vat of acid, not even knowing what acid is, you will not want to place your hand in it.

The difference between fear and disgust is that while fear was created as an automatic response to immediate danger, with a systemic fight or flight response, disgust must be deduced with reasoning: A+B=C, and you really don't want C to happen.

Since disgust must be learned, it is also an emotion very susceptible to conjecture, falsehoods, and fallacies. This can cause real damage when we are taught that certain good things are bad or that certain things that pose no threat are evil.

It is how a parent's neurosis, bad food habits, or even racism and bigotry can be passed on from generation to generation. This is because it is an emotion that when developed, makes us wary of things or people that appear different, or things that resemble something taught as potentially dangerous or unknown.

The beautiful thing about disgust is that knowledge is power. What can be learned can be unlearned. Again, cognitive behavioral therapy can be of great benefit to a person with the severe, learned neurosis of this kind.

I know some of you can get a little weary when talking about unlearning things, however, I am only speaking of clear, undeniable, unarguable falsehoods. I am certainly not talking about Orwellian re-education.

As humans in the modern world, we tend to overreact to potential threats, especially legal ones.

Corporate sensitivity training, while having great potential to educate people in a healthy way, also poses the biggest threat of overstepping those boundaries, into the kind of re-education that leads us to a less free and ultimately less fulfilling society. We must be very careful not to go too far, sticking only to indisputable facts while designing courses such as these.

Racism and bigotry are inarguably the most harmful byproduct of the learned/taught emotion of disgust in our modern world.

When humanity was developing, there were valid reasons to be wary of others outside of your own tribe. Therefore disgust/fear of others was taught and passed down by our forebears. Warfare was common amongst even neighboring tribes around the world and posed a real, physical threat to you and your family. Even though their similarities far outweighed their differences.

Even in modern times, racism is not simply based on skin color, culture, or language. It's not a white thing, a black thing, a brown thing or a yellow thing.

It has never been that simple, for the reasons I just explained. You hear a lot about gang violence in big cities like Chicago.

These gangs are simply derivatives of tribes of the past. Many fighting each other over territory or retribution for one slight against the other.

They can only be stopped once we are able to openly talk about the breakdown of the family unit within these communities.

If a child's needs are being fulfilled by their family, strong examples being given by two parents, they have no need to look outward to criminal organizations.

I lived in South America in my early 20's, Ecuador to be exact. I found it interesting to see the racism between people of the highlands, Quito and people from the coast, Guayaquil in such a small country.

By most accounts, they are racially and culturally very similar and speak the same language. Even with all their commonalities, people from the highlands would derogatorily call people from the coast, "Monos de la costa" or, "Monkeys of the coast."

In Europe and parts of the USA, white on white racism is common between people in different regions. Even neighboring countries. It also happens in Asia between Asians, Africa between Africans and basically, all over the world.

Unfortunately, as we have grown more civilized, this learned emotion, when used in racism/bigotry has not yet completely died out in our world.

It has grown less than any other time in history, especially in the western world, though will likely take a few more generations of relative harmony to rid completely.

To live in this relative harmony, people must try to interact respectfully with each other. Be kind to each other. Positive interaction between people of different ethnic and cultural backgrounds tends to point out our commonalities and bring us together.

It teaches us naturally, that even though a person may look or sound different, we are more similar than we appear. This is the most effective way of bridging the cultural gap.

The human instinct for comfort and familiarity unfortunately still leads us to congregate in communities with people who share similar cultural and ethnic backgrounds.

I grew up in California's Silicon Valley and watched as it turned into one of the most ethnically and culturally diverse places on the planet. I also watched people of all different cultural and ethnic backgrounds interact well together during the day, working together, having lunch, forming friendships but then retreating to their micro-communities made up of people with similar ethnic and cultural backgrounds.

Time has historically been a great solution to this problem and along with daily interaction, I hope it will continue to be.

Likewise, the least effective way is through forced re-education. Where if you don't outwardly and immediately subscribe to whatever the in-vogue terminology of the day is, you are treated as a pariah. This does nothing but create resistance and ironically has the opposite of its intended effect.

People of good heart and no ill intention are afraid of being labeled a racist or bigot for a simple sleight of the tongue. Real solutions to societal problems are not being addressed or talked about, for fear of not being politically correct.

When you are forced into recognizing people's differences over their commonalities, to treat people differently due to historical marginalization, it does nothing to bring people together today. Furthermore, nearly every cultural group throughout history has been marginalized, at some point, by another cultural group.

To live a fulfilling life, you must learn to let go of negative emotions from things that no longer physically affect you or from situations you have no ability to change.

In the case of historical marginalization and slavery, most people directly affected by it have long passed away.

For those still alive during the Jim Crow era, you have a legitimate reason to have felt marginalized because you were. However, like much of the Japanese that were placed in camps during WW2, you have likely moved on and made peace with past errors. You have not let those negative experiences define who you are.

You cannot change your skin color or ethnicity and you cannot change the past. You can only choose to not let the past mistakes of others dictate your present, your future and how fulfilling your life will be.

When I started writing about the prime emotion of disgust, I did not have the intention of writing so much about racism, besides its historical relevance and how it came to be. It is talked about a lot in the society today, more than I can remember in my nearly 40 years. Our differences have somehow, over the past decade, become more relevant than our commonalities.

To live a truly fulfilling life, we must come together as a society, work together, help each other and appreciate the things that make us all human, not separate beings.

I will write a few more paragraphs on this subject because it is one more solution to this complex issue. One of the 36 rules to a fulfilling life is to travel as often as you can.

If you do not live in an ethnically diverse community, world travel is an excellent way to get this natural experience. I'm not talking about posting up in your 4 or 5-star resort, where you only interact with the staff and other tourists.

I'm talking about real travel where you experience cultures, food and people that look, live and sound different than those familiar to you.

Think of the television shows hosted by one of my own personal icons, the late Anthony Bourdain. (Not to go off on too much of a tangent but his untimely suicide is an excellent example to reference. No matter how much money you have or how great of a career you hold, there can still be great unfulfillment in your life. So much so that one can overcome our greatest instinct, the instinct of survival. Even in a man who was as seeming wise as he.)

If you are observant and open to new experiences, a requirement for a truly fulfilling life, you might just bring back a gem or two of wisdom, different than your original way of thinking.

This is not cultural appropriation, this is cultural appreciation. Taking the good things from many different cultures and blending them together was the recipe that made the United States so successful in the first place.

EMOTION 6 - TRUST:

When used in an emotional context, trust is defined as: firm belief in the reliability, truth, ability, or strength of someone or something.

I am asking for a great deal of your trust as readers of this book. I ask that while you may not agree with everything I say, that you trust in following the 36 rules to a fulfilling life and that they will work for you.

Trust is something that must be earned, which is why I am providing you with as much information and context as possible, without providing so many statistics that you lose interest.

My hope is that by doing this, you will believe that I am truly trying to help you live a more fulfilling life and to provide the world with a little more good.

Hopefully, I am also doing so in a way that makes sense to you. Hopefully, you believe that I hold the knowledge and have researched the information I am writing about. That this book is not just one big pile of bullshit.

I said trust is something that must be earned but that is not the full truth. I'm sure many of you caught onto this and began to lose faith in my knowledge, to lose trust in me and this book. I did this to prove just how fragile trust can be and that once you have it, you hold a great responsibility to keep it.

Trust can be earned or it can be inherent. The greatest example of inherent trust is what a baby feels towards its parents, even seconds after taking his or her first breath.

Trust is a wonderful emotion. To have full and complete trust in another is having full and complete trust that you will be taken care of, no matter what. That this person who holds your trust will not deceive you, will never intentionally hurt you and will hold their interests to the same standards as your own.

It is a warm, comfortable feeling to experience complete trust. It is also easy to see why Dr. Plutchik described love as a combination of joy and trust.

Some people choose to trust others immediately and give them the benefit of the doubt until proven untrustworthy. Other people are more skeptical and slow to trust. A lot of this difference is based on their own, individual life experiences.

The basis for this generally starts in early childhood, as babies. If their parents can regularly fulfill their needs, the baby's ability to grow and develop the emotion of trust strengthens.

Likewise, if a baby's parents do not fulfill their basic needs, the child will generally grow up with a multitude of trust and behavioral issues, even when interacting with good, trustworthy people, many years later.

One's ease in trusting others in a normal way is shaped as they grow from children to adults. If someone has had their trust broken repeatedly, this creates wounds to the soul.

These wounds hurt and can be difficult to heal. Depending upon the severity and frequency, these wounds may heal completely or turn into massive scars, acting like an exoskeleton or the shell of a turtle. This shell then becomes a protection mechanism, making it more difficult to penetrate, more difficult to trust. They consciously and/or subconsciously want to avoid becoming hurt again.

We have already mentioned several times, trust is one of two primary emotions needed to feel love.

The emotion of love is arguably the most important emotion in a life fulfilled. Therefore, we must take great care with the trust of other people and never intentionally break the trust of others. Especially of those you care about.

If you are having issues with trusting others, start making baby steps. While there are bad people in this world, most of us are pretty good. To live a fulfilling life, you need to be able to trust others just as others need to be able to trust in you.

There are plenty of books you can read that specifically address this and professional therapy may help you find the root of the problem more quickly. You must, however, find a way to work through this and working through the 36 rules to fulfillment will certainly help.

You don't have to dive straight in, just start by dipping your toes in the water. I think you may find that the more of these rules you live by, the more you will learn to trust others, just as others will learn to trust in you.

EMOTION 7 - ANTICIPATION:

Anticipation is a feeling of expectation based on the prediction of a future event.

This could be based upon an actual, prior experience, like waking up on Christmas morning to a tree surrounded by presents.

This could also be a visualization of what you presume an experience will be like in your mind due to something you may have heard or seen. You can feel the anticipation before anything that happens, whether positive or negative, real or imagined.

Anticipation is one of two emotions that can be either positive or negative; A help or a hindrance on the path to fulfillment. At the heart of anticipation is a feeling of energy.

This energy is typically either exciting and happy, like planning for a vacation or nervous and unsettling, like sitting in wait for an important job interview. Another word for this feeling, when used in a negative context is anxiety.

Excluding generalized anxiety disorder or certain conditions that revolve around the anticipation of terrible things, one should learn to harness anticipation. It comes easier to some depending on the situation.

A quick fix many new public speakers use as a crutch, before becoming comfortable with public speaking is a class of medication, known as beta blockers. These are typically blood pressure medications but some have also been known to help ease the outward signs of nervous energy.

They have banned these drugs in shooting competitions because they provide such a strong edge, steadying the hands of the shooter while keeping the mind clear.

I am not a Medical Doctor and I am in no way advising or advertising the use of such a medication for such a purpose. My goal is to teach you the 36 rules to a fulfilling life and each of the 36 rules listed is completely natural. The use of beta blockers for the above purpose is somewhat common knowledge and another quick fix solution, so for that reason, I felt compelled to mention it.

When you are anticipating something fun, something positive, there is no need to change that feeling. Why would you want to? I can think of one reason and that is setting unrealistic expectations. If your anticipation is not based in reality, even when it is positive, you are setting yourself up for disappointment.

However, when I write of learning to harness anticipation, I am speaking more about learning to harness the nervous energy or anxiety that anticipation creates to naturally strengthen your performance.

Luckily, anticipation is one of the easiest emotions to learn control over and use to your benefit.

Physical exercise probably helps the best. If you are an athlete, you already know how to harness that anticipation before an important race or big game. I used to race mountain bikes competitively and as I lined up on my bike, alongside the other racers, I was almost shaking with nervous energy. Then went the bang of the starting gun and I felt my body take over. All those nerves, all of that energy made me explode through the starting gate with more power than I thought I had in me.

Whether or not you are an athlete, before you know it, you are in the middle of doing what you were anticipating and should then trust in your skill, preparation, and practice. Don't further anticipate something bad happening. Just trust in yourself and do what you do.

Meditation is a great tool to calm the nerves of anticipation. If you don't know how to or aren't a meditator, simply try to distract yourself for a moment by thinking of a good time that you had in the past. For this to work, you must try and remember every little detail and picture it as accurately as possible. This doesn't last forever because at some point, you must return to the moment, but is a helpful tip.

The biggest factor in controlling how anticipation makes you feel is to prepare yourself, set realistic expectations, visualize how you would like it to be and; know that things will rarely go according to plan but you must persevere.

EMOTION 8 - SURPRISE:

Surprise is defined as the feeling caused by something unexpected or unusual. I think the key word here is "unexpected" because if we are expecting something unusual, we are less likely to feel surprised by it. Most of the time anyway.

There are good surprises in life and there are bad surprises in life. To throw a wrench in the mix, sometimes what we initially think of as good surprises turn out to be bad and the bad surprises turn out to be amazingly good. Ironically, one thing you can always count on is that you will be surprised from time to time.

Everyone deals with surprise differently. Some people love them no matter what and some even hate the good ones. I happen to fall into the latter category by nature, though sometimes I'll even surprise myself and enjoy them.

There are some things in life that you are expecting to happen. You even anticipate how you will feel emotionally when they happen... Then BAM!!! You are completely surprised that it happened, when it happened, why it happened and especially how you felt about it after it happened. This is something often seen with the death of a close, chronically ill family member.

As much as I say I hate them, what would life really be like without surprises? If given the option of knowing how my life will play out to the exact detail, every minute of every day or not knowing a damn thing about my future, I'll choose door number two every time. Life would be tirelessly boring without surprises, even the ones that don't seem so great at first.

Start living by the 36 rules to a fulfilling life, even the hard ones... especially the hard ones and I'll bet you'll look back at yourself one year from today and be utterly surprised at just how much more fulfilling your life has become. How much your life has changed for the better.

Do me a favor, mark that day on your calendar and when it arrives, do a little honest self-reflection. When you are done, please don't forget to send me an update. I would really love to hear about all the positive change that has manifested in your life.

SECTION 3: THE TOP 8 SHORTCUTS TO HAPPINESS / VICES / INDISCRETIONS AND WHY THEY RARELY LEAD TO FULFILMENT

I have already spoken of some of the top shortcuts to happiness/vices/indiscretions during the chapters on challenges to fulfillment and understanding the 8 primary human emotions. Social media and video games, being two that are often abused.

I could write an entire encyclopedia on vices, shortcuts to happiness and indiscretions but will only concentrate on a few. This is after all, a guide to fulfillment, not away from it.

There are a few shortcuts to happiness that when used in moderation, may not hinder your path to fulfillment. The path to fulfillment is like an epic journey that never ends - a collection of actions, experiences, and choices made throughout your entire life.

You will not see the magnitude of its importance until you are well on your way, or you are way off its path. Luckily, it is never too late and you are never too far off your path to change course and gain fulfillment.

There are no shortcuts to fulfillment but there are many shortcuts to happiness, or at least a chemical response mimicking happiness.

All shortcuts to happiness are short-lived but may hold some positive benefits when used in moderation and for the right reasons.

When used in this way, they may aid in creating experiences necessary for a fulfilling life. With that being said, they are almost always unfulfilling, even if fun at the time.

Many shortcuts are clearly destructive and dangerous, even in small doses. All shortcuts and vices are destructive when taken to the extreme or not used in moderation.

Moderation is clearly the key here as some of these listed as shortcuts to happiness are 100% necessary to biological life, like eating food.

I feel like I must also put a disclaimer in for legal reasons before I start this section: I am in no way condoning the use of any illegal or legal substances when used illegally. Nor am I advising in the participation of any listed or non-listed illegal activities, whether written here or anywhere else in this book.

I have made my views clear on the 36 rules to fulfillment and none of the following shortcuts/vices/indiscretions are specified within them.

If you choose to partake in any of them other than eating for biological necessity or infrequently shopping for basic items needed to sustain life such as simple clothing and shelter, that responsibility is solely on you, the reader.

It is your life and I will not judge you, just as you should try your best not to judge others.

You are reading this book to gain more fulfillment in your life. Sometimes you may not even realize you are participating in an activity hindering fulfillment. This happens often and will usually need to be pointed out. I will try to be as honest and forthcoming as possible, just as I have promised while writing this entire book.

I will not only list the shortcuts, vices, and indiscretions but also list what makes them attractive, along with potential pitfalls.

As I mentioned, this list is not all-inclusive or exhaustive. I only felt it necessary to list the most frequent shortcuts/vices/indiscretions I see people taking.

The last three are those with almost no positivity except in the most extreme circumstances. They are indiscretions that are quite simply immoral.

I'm sure you learned all about them as a child and why they are wrong. However, we still engage in them as a society because they have the potential to be a shortcut to our own selfish wants. That is why they are listed here.

NUMBER 1 - ALCOHOL:

It is legal in most countries in the world, easily accessible and as cheap or expensive as you are willing to pay.

It can be viewed as a status symbol for the rich, a way to unwind after a long day at work, a social lubricant helpful in making the introverted a little more outgoing, a delicious, magical elixir to turn a boring activity fun or make the good times even better.

It can also be viewed as the shackles, binding an addict to a life of reliance and misery, a gateway to more harmful substances, the syrup of vagrants, the lifeblood of the homeless and most downtrodden members of society.

As you can see, alcohol has quite a range. When used in moderation, it does little harm.

There are even studies showing how regular consumption of small amounts of certain alcoholic beverages can be beneficial to your health.

Although as with anything else, there are now studies refuting those previous studies. Science can be funny that way and most times, it's best to just use common sense.

My take on alcohol is that it is something to be enjoyed, though not too often. I relish in tasting a fine wine, especially pinot noir from the Santa Ynez Valley. I have spent many days roaming wine country and have been a member of many different wineries throughout the years.

I also enjoy sipping on a glass of whiskey (Scotch or Irish but not Bourbon).

Then again, it doesn't get much better than a tropical, fruity confection served in a fresh coconut shell while on an island retreat.

There are three rules I try and set with alcohol. Do not drink out of anger/sadness, do not drink by myself and do not drink too often.

I'm pretty good at following them, most of the time and these rules have worked well for me thus far. When I do drink by myself, it's usually just one glass of something.

As far as frequency, I usually partake only once, maybe twice a week at most.

Full disclosure, some of these rules, particularly pertaining to frequency fly out of the window while I'm on vacation. Hey, I'm only human!

I am also not fooling myself into thinking that drinking alcohol, as enjoyable as it can be, helps lead to a fulfilling life.

If any true fulfillment is gained while drinking alcohol (not just momentary, chemically induced happiness), it is not the alcohol that creates fulfillment.

The fulfillment comes from the people I am spending time with, the other activities being performed and/or the location I am in.

Therefore, while alcohol is meant to be enjoyed responsibly, it is not meant to solve any of your problems or better your life in any way.

It can be one of the most dangerous shortcuts to happiness because like any other drug, it makes you feel better almost immediately and it works like that most of the time. It also clouds your judgment and can lead to some really bad decisions. Decisions that may not just negatively impact you but others as well.

Alcohol kills thousands of innocent people every year by drunk drivers, violence and alcohol related health complications.

If you have a problem with alcohol, an addiction that is interfering with your life or especially if causing harm to the lives of others, please seek help.

At this point, it has become a potentially fatal disease. Without professional treatment, you are risking the lives of others as well as your own. That is anything but fulfilling.

NUMBER 2 - DRUGS/PHARMACEUTICALS:

We talked a little about certain drugs and how they impact the body during the section on emotions. I will rehash it here in greater depth because drugs and pharmaceutical usage are one of the fastest and most widely used shortcuts to happiness.

Let me first speak to the legal use of prescribed pharmaceuticals. You cannot deny that they help a lot of people. We have life-saving treatments never thought possible because of breakthroughs in the pharmaceutical industry. People are living longer and more mobile lives due to these breakthroughs.

Advancement in medicine is a wonderful and miraculous thing. When you are unwell, when your body feels physically unwell, it is very difficult to maintain or add to a fulfilling life.

There are also many prescribed pharmaceuticals legitimately treating people with severe mental health issues.

I have seen firsthand what untreated, severe mental illness looks like. I have also seen the change, for the better in those same people, when being properly treated with prescribed pharmaceuticals.

For these people, behavioral psychotherapy is not even a possibility unless they are complying with their medications.

There people with severe depression, generalized anxiety disorder, panic disorder, PTSD, OCD and many other conditions that ultimately benefit from the prescription pharmaceutical industry.

I will never make an argument against the proper use of prescription medication when it is truly needed. Many doctors also recommend cognitive behavioral therapy, combined with these medications to receive the full benefit.

Now again, I am not a Medical Doctor, though many Medical Doctors have agreed that there is a crisis of over-prescription today. There are many reasons for this and I'm not necessarily blaming MDs.

The pharmaceutical industry is in business to make money and like any business, will flood the market with advertisements and other marketing efforts to sell more and more products. They will offer solutions to problems you didn't even realize you had, until now.

People also have more access to complex but simplified medical information than ever before. They know they feel bad and want to feel better fast. Everyone is looking for that quick fix, silver bullet to whatever problem ails them.

They then take that information with them to their doctor's office and know exactly what to say to get a prescription for that quick fix, a chemical band-aid to a problem they could cure, with a little more, actual effort.

This is especially true when speaking of mental health and weight loss. I'm certainly not discounting the fact that there are more unhappy people today than years past.

There are plenty of charts, poles and studies to prove this to be true. It is my theory however, that lifestyle is largely to blame in most of these people trying to improve their lives with pharmaceuticals.

I am also hearing theories that diet alone, has the potential to cure depression in some people. Serotonin, created primarily in the digestive tract as having something to do with this.

The whole reasoning behind this book is to help people, specifically these people live better, more fulfilling lives, in a natural way. If you need to use prescription medications as a crutch, while you put in the real work to change your life for the better, to make it fulfilling, by all means, go talk to your doctor about it.

The illegal/improper usage of prescription pharmaceuticals is very much more concerning. They are powerful drugs, some with a high propensity for addiction.

Not only that, many of these medications can be deadly when mixed. The blended use of opioids, benzodiazepines, and alcohol are responsible for a huge number of accidental deaths by overdose.

The bottom line with prescriptions, if you think you need them, go talk with your doctor and make sure they know the truth about everything you are taking.

Even herbal medications and vitamins. Some are very powerful and contain ingredients contraindicated with other medications. Also, if you have been abusing certain medications, talk to your Doctor about the best way to quit.

Some substances can be deadly to stop cold turkey, like alcohol and benzodiazepines, unless proper protocols are put into place.

Now onto the fun stuff! I'm joking / half joking here of course. There are certain other drugs that may be illegal federally but legal or decriminalized for recreational use in your city or state. Marijuana is the big one here.

As I write this, the city of Denver just voted to decriminalize the use of magic mushrooms. That will certainly be an interesting experiment.

While all drugs, especially unregulated ones hold the potential to cause addiction and great physical harm, it would be disingenuous to say the risk is equal across the board.

Now, remember, like alcohol, none of these will cause you to have a fulfilling life. If you choose to use them, know going-in the risk you are taking and use them in moderation. There are also certain drugs you must never try if you ever want to have a realistic chance at a fulfilling life.

The best you can hope for is a short, happy experience with little negative consequence. Marijuana, in legal, regulated areas is clearly the safest option when it comes to federally illegal drugs.

It is typically highly regulated by its respective state, so you know exactly what you are buying, what is in it and exactly how strong the dose is that you are taking. Some people say marijuana is a medication and a safer option than alcohol, while others state that regular, high dose usage can lead to psychosis, specifically schizophrenia.

The reality is, to the people who call it medication, we just don't have enough data yet to say how beneficial it is. Does it carry greater or lesser risks than other, more studied pharmaceuticals.

To those of you who admittedly use it for purely recreational purposes, because we have specific cannabinoid receptors in our brain that when stimulated make us feel good, use it responsibly, please. Moderation is important. It will also not make your life more fulfilled on its own.

Like alcohol, it is the social situations and experiences created, while you happen to be using it that can aid in real life fulfillment.

Drugs you must never try are heroin, methamphetamine aka crystal meth, crack and the improper or un-prescribed use of prescription opioids and benzodiazepines. They are far too addictive and far too dangerous to risk your life on.

I'm not saying that the experience you feel in the moment won't be better than anything you have ever felt in your life. Quite the opposite is what I am afraid of.

A chemically created illusion played on your mind, so good that you are willing to ruin your life, relationships with everyone you care about and even die just to experience. In my mind, nothing is that good.

I don't think the numbers of people using PCP are as high as the others but that's another one I would recommend staying away from. My experiences as a Paramedic, with people using it, have never been very positive.

I don't know enough about any other drugs to give you much advice besides to be careful if you do indulge and none of them will do anything to make your life any better.

I've seen some people dabble safely here and there with powdered cocaine while others spiral into full-blown addiction, nearly losing their lives.

If you do choose to experiment with any substance, please educate yourself first and know with certainty what you are putting into your body. Also, consider the legal ramifications and costs associated if you are caught with an illegal substance.

What I really recommend, if you must indulge, is to wait until you are very old, have already lived a fulfilling life and feel dementia starting to set in before you try the really dangerous ones.

At that point, get your affairs in order, say goodbye to your loved ones, buy a sailboat, and all the drugs you want, even meth, crack and heroin, then sail off into the sunset, knowing full well that you will most likely never return.

NUMBER 3 - SHOPPING:

When I speak to shopping as a negative in the shortcut to happiness, I am speaking of two things. An addiction to shopping and materialism.

There is nothing wrong with wanting to own nice things. A nice house in a great neighborhood or luxuries designed to make your life more comfortable are indulgences I enjoy. In fact, they can be very motivational when it comes to putting in the work necessary to earn them.

Just buy them for the right reasons and make sure you can afford whatever it happens to be. Never shop just to make someone else jealous or to "Keep up with the Jones".

Will nice things make your life more fulfilled? Some may if you can afford them; like a nice home in a great neighborhood with excellent schools for your children to attend.

By the same token, it can also make you more stressed out, just trying to pay your mortgage. Others might make mundane tasks a little more enjoyable or life a little more comfortable.

When you buy your first luxury automobile, you can feel the quality and craftsmanship almost every time you drive it. The smell of the leather. The silence of the cabin or the clarity of the sound system. You can feel the power of the engine, the smoothness of the transmission and the superior handling immediately. You think to yourself, "This is really living!"

Then, something slowly starts to happen. Something that happens with all possessions over time. You stop appreciating the things that initially impressed you. Your beautiful BMW, Infinity, Jaguar or Porsche just starts to become, "Your car". You know, that thing you slump into and fight traffic with every day to and from work.

This happens with furniture, clothing, jewelry and to some extent, even your home (why people tend to trade up every few years) ... Basically, anything you can buy will lose a little of what made it so special to you, over time.

Therefore, you should never try to gain fulfillment with shopping and materialism. You must keep buying more, bigger and better things to get the same feeling you had with your first, whatever it was.

Shopping can also be a legitimate addiction, sending families into financial ruin. It stimulates all the same feel-good hormones you get with drugs and alcohol.

You literally feel, "High" when buying something new. Nearly everyone feels that to some extent, especially when you are finally able to buy something you've wanted for a long time.

Think of someone with the physical need to have that feeling all the time. That is what I mean when talking about a shopping addiction. This is especially true when you start to feel financial pain from it. That should be your first clue a problem may be developing. If ignored, you can expect to go down the same path as someone with any other addiction until you realize the problem and seek out treatment to fix it.

Look, I am no one to tell you that you shouldn't buy nice things, when you can. Always pay for quality on something you plan to keep for a while or use regularly.

I own a bigger house than I probably need, on the top of a hillside, in one of the most beautiful, private neighborhoods in the country.

I can honestly tell you that when driving between the break in the mountains, around the corner, past the gate, and into my neighborhood, I literally feel my body destress from the natural beauty.

I can also say that while still a financial liability, with a mortgage, it will continue to be and has already become an excellent investment.

Without turning this into a book on real estate strategy, always try to purchase your home in as close to any naturally occurring, geographically beautiful place you can afford (Man-made beauty or job-centric area would be your next choices).

Not only does it provide a physical barrier against building more homes (aka adding inventory), it will always be a desirable place for people to live. Who doesn't love a beautiful view or a short commute? If you can afford both, that's the creme de la creme of residential real estate investing.

All I am saying is to never place more value on material possessions than your relationships with others. Also, if you find yourself shopping

57

to make yourself feel good, "Therapeutic shopping" a little too often, you may be developing or have already developed a shopping addiction. You will never find fulfillment this way. Momentary happiness maybe, though like everything else, you must eventually pay the bill.

Like many people from my generation, I find experiences more valuable than physical things. Your car will eventually get old but you'll always remember that special trip you took with your friends, family or spouse.

Not only will you have that memory for a lifetime, but you will also have seen and tried new things, learned something and gained a little more perspective than you had before.

Experiences almost always lead to a more fulfilling life. Just make sure you can meet your basic needs, try to save for the future and not put those experiences on credit.

NUMBER 4 - FOOD:

You need food to survive, everyone does. In and of itself, this is not a shortcut to happiness, vice or indiscretion, it's a biological necessity needed to sustain life itself.

There are two ways that food can become shortcuts and vices however: Emotional overeating or to the contrary, depriving your body of necessary nutrients due to conditions like anorexia and bulimia.

If I haven't emphasized it enough already and you're not seeing the trend of moderation, you might as well put this book down because you're not paying attention.

I'm no dietary expert, that's for certain. I'm not a picture of perfect physical fitness but I'm in relatively decent shape. There are so many diets and food fads out there, many saying completely contradicting things. It truly amazes me.

Notwithstanding legitimate hormone issues, staying fit basically boils down to two things, take in fewer calories than you burn if trying to lose weight or keep them balanced to maintain weight.

It is really that simple and most people are just not active enough. Stay active throughout your life. Your body will thank you and it just feels good.

Look at the farmers of the past. They ate terribly fatty, high calorie, high carbohydrate foods but were active, burning off those calories and carbs all day, every day.

That is why they all look so skinny in the photos you see. They also had the benefit of whole, unprocessed, organic foods, which provided them with many more essential nutrients than what you find in your average grocery store now. That is improving luckily, as well as the prices for most organic foods.

It's not surprising that the less fulfilled a person's life is, the more they try and replace it with a full belly. I'm not trying to be insensitive. It's a proven fact that some people turn to food during emotionally tough times.

When faced with negative emotions, many people will binge eat, not even tasting or really enjoying their food. They also tend to turn to whatever is the most convenient and the most convenient foods, typically are not the healthiest. Most tend to gain overeating habits as food becomes tied to their emotions, whether consciously or subconsciously.

There are several things you can do to break this habit. It's not easy and some of the advice is like a smoker trying to quit. Again, this is no diet book and there are plenty of resources specifically aimed at helping you stop emotional eating. Here are a few though:

When you feel the urge to eat due to an emotional stressor, go outside for a brief walk. It will help take your mind off the severity of the emotional stressor and your body will also receive a positive boost of endorphins. Those endorphins also act as a natural appetite suppressant.

You should also buy healthful foods when you go to the grocery store and try to limit purchases of easy to prepare, unhealthful foods. Fruit is a great substitution and an easy, relatively healthy snack to grab when the urge strikes. I heard a tip once that when shopping at a grocery store, stick to the perimeter and don't go down the aisles. The perimeter is usually where the healthier, fresher foods are.

The other problem with food is due to the lack of it. Anorexia and bulimia are dangerous, potentially deadly, physical and psychological disorders.

If you suffer from either of these conditions, please see a doctor about them right away. They will provide you with the treatment that you urgently need. Both disorders also have one thing in common. It's an unhealthy focus/view on the self.

Start following the 36 rules to a fulfilling life, while receiving professional, medical care and you will start to notice your life turning around for the better.

NUMBER 5 - GAMBLING:

You may be noticing a trend here with each shortcut to happiness/vice I have listed so far. They all stimulate areas of the brain responsible for releasing feel-good hormones and chemicals.

Gambling creates a very strong dopamine release when making a bet and an even stronger serotonin release if that bet is won.

There also lies the potential in every role of the dice or pull of the slot machine handle to get rich quick. To change your life completely with just a little bit of luck. Even though the odds are stacked incredibly against you, people still win sometimes.

That's the same idea behind the lottery, somebody will always win and damn it, why can't that someone be you? It can, it's not impossible, however small the odds may be. That's what keeps people coming back to the casinos or buying lottery tickets, day after day.

It can be fun to gamble, when done in a healthy way, in moderation. When loss limits are set and you can go into the casino with the intention to win but knowing full well that you will not be hurt if/when you lose.

Even the luckiest of the lucky, like my grandmother, who seems to win every time she steps foot in a casino, doesn't win all the time.

The trick is to not look at your loss as a loss of money but the cost of entertainment. The cost of giving yourself that dream of potential riches. That can be fun and money well spent, in and of itself. Also, never forget, the casino wouldn't be in business is it gave out more money than it took in.

If you were one of the "Lucky" ones that win some grand fortune, that will not by itself make you fulfilled.

I'm guessing you would at first feel shocked and overwhelming happiness but those feelings will eventually fade. They always do, especially when that something comes easily to you.

The curse of the lottery is a real thing. While it doesn't touch all lottery winners, it will chew up and spit out those not living an actual, fulfilling life.

I recently went to a duck derby at a local festival with my wife and son. We "bought" five rubber ducks to join in the racing fun.

The grand price was a few thousand dollars and I thought maybe, I might have a shot at winning something. After all, how many ducks could you sell at a local festival?

We made our way to the creek where I saw about 10,000 rubber ducks. Watching them all float down the river, the overwhelming number, really put those 300 million:1 lottery odds into perspective. We didn't even come close to winning anything.

Our closest duck was more than 1000 ducks off. That wasn't the point luckily. I wasn't trying to win money to pay my mortgage.

Spending time with my family on a beautiful day, getting to see how excited my son was watching all the ducks... that was prize enough.

Like every vice and potential shortcut to happiness, there lies the potential for it to turn into a lifelong addiction. This addiction can bankrupt people from all walks of life. People have literally been killed for the inability to pay back their gambling losses.

There is help and aside from trying to live your life by the 36 rules to fulfillment, join a support group like Gamblers Anonymous.

The first step is realizing you have a problem and that is usually the hardest one to take.

NUMBER 6 - LYING:

Lying will almost always lead you away from the path to fulfillment, with a few exceptions. Small white lies told to save the feelings of someone else are usually not destructive and sometimes almost expected.

If your family or friends invite you over for dinner but the food was overcooked or otherwise not up to your taste, telling them, "Thank you" and that you liked it will generally do no harm.

Most people know when they have overcooked something. I know when I do. However, I still appreciate the sentiment of a guest telling me they liked something I made, even when I know it's probably not true.

The same goes for other small things that people cannot change and the lie is only used to save their feelings or boost their confidence. "Oh wow, you look great in that outfit" is one I think we've all said a time or two and not meant it.

Never lie about anything big. Develop a reputation as someone of character. That is hard to do once you have been caught in a whopper or series of lies. A lot of the time, it might feel easier to lie than to tell the truth.

Maybe you stand to lose something by telling the truth. While you might lose something, or have some consequence by telling the truth, you will certainly damage your character and lose the trust of another by lying when you are caught.

In other words, you always have a better chance not to lose with the truth, than the certainty of losing it with a lie.

Most people have a hard time lying and it shows through their body language. I have received training on how to spot a lie and people are way more transparent than they think. It also hurts most of us to lie because most of us naturally have a decent moral character.

There are those that have no problem lying and do not feel remorseful at all. They are known as psychopaths and true psychopathy is real and luckily, rare.

Ironically there are probably more true psychopaths in powerful positions than we would like to admit. However, they will never be able to experience a truly fulfilling life as their inability to feel remorse also limits their ability to feel other emotions. Good emotions. For this, we should have sympathy for them.

There is one other exception where it is 100% acceptable to lie. No matter how big the lie is. That is if you, our those you love are in danger. To save yourself or other people, like a hostage situation or kidnapping, something along those lines.

In those situations, say whatever it is you need to say to stay alive.

NUMBER 7 - CHEATING:

I will use the Merriam-Webster definition here so there are no questions about the exact meaning. *What the definition of is, is.* Cheating can be defined as a transitive and intransitive verb. I will define them both:

Transitive verb: 1: To deprive something valuable by the use of deceit or fraud. 2: To influence or lead by deceit, trick or artifice. 3: To elude or thwart by or as if by outwitting.

Intransitive Verb: 1: To practice fraud or trickery - to violate rules dishonestly. 2: to be sexually unfaithful. 3: To position oneself defensively near a particular area in anticipation of a play in that area.

I think we can all agree that just about every definition, except for potentially two, are immoral, unethical and maybe even illegal. The first that stands out as potentially not harmful to a fulfilling life is transitive verb definition 3: To elude or thwart by or as outwitting. If this is done in an upfront and honest way, it is practically the point of every board game, sports game, battle, etc. The second is intransitive verb 3: To position oneself defensively near a particular area in anticipation of a play in that area. Unless the rules in whatever activity or game specifically prohibit this, it is just plain, good strategy.

When used in any other way, cheating will never lead to a fulfilling life. Sure, it may lead to quick riches but it may also lead to a long prison sentence.

It may lead to a bevy of sexual partners but if you're in a relationship, it can also lead to the loss of that relationship. More importantly, the loss of trust from the person you care about in that relationship.

Cheating is basically just another way of lying but with a form of action.

Like lying, there are no rules when your life is in danger but otherwise, you have more to lose by cheating than you stand to gain.

If you live your life in a moral and ethical way, as someone known for their character, you will still rise to the top. It may take a little longer but you will rise in a way that is truly fulfilling and truly earned.

The top is also classified differently for everyone. Just as what might be fun to you may be boring to me, the top for you may be financial, developmental, relationship-based or some mixture of it all.

NUMBER 8 - STEALING:

Stealing is one shortcut to financial gain that many unfulfilled people take. A shortcut taken by those who may have never learned the 36 rules to a fulfilling life or by those who have intentionally ignored them.

Stealing is also something that most of us have done at one point or another. Maybe you took a piece of candy from a store as a child or a pack of cigarettes from a store as a teenager. Whatever it was, you were probably caught by someone and taught why it is wrong.

Theft may be on a small or grand scale and can take on many different forms. It may come from dumb kids, street thugs, gangs, business owners, the occasional bored celebrity (Looking at you Winona! Timely reference I know), corporate leaders and Wall Street tycoons.

I'm not here to lecture you about why stealing is wrong and how it will not lead to a fulfilling life. If you didn't already know that, you probably wouldn't be reading this book in the first place.

The only exception I see where it is not as bad is when someone is only stealing a necessity to survive.

Even then, notwithstanding disaster or other rare circumstances, there are generally government programs in place or charities that should render it unnecessary.

Many of the 36 rules to fulfillment have been learned either through my own successes and mistakes or by observing the successes and mistakes of others throughout history.

I try to live a good life and practice what I preach. I am also not writing another version of the bible and am no saint, not by any means.

I also promised to be honest and open with you which is why I am including this story:

I remember trying to steal a few bottles of alcohol from the grocery store as a teenager. I was caught, well technically named and then turned myself in after the fact. I was brought to the store by my father and given the chance to apologize to the store manager.

My father then drove me to the Sheriff's office so I could turn myself in. I spoke with the Sheriff and was genuinely remorseful for my actions. I was not just remorseful for being caught. Luckily, the store manager could hear this in my voice and called the Sheriff's office prior to my arrival, asking not to press charges or file any kind of official report.

I was not a good criminal and generally a pretty good kid. Luckily, I learned this lesson early in life.

Clearly, I learned that what I did was wrong. That even though it was a big store, that could technically afford to lose a few bottles of alcohol, that didn't make it right. Not to mention the fact that I was underage.

I also learned that the store accounts for people stealing and in turn, raises prices on everything for everyone because of it. I hadn't thought about the good, law-abiding people who could barely afford their groceries, having to pay more because of the actions of people like me.

In the end, I like to think that society will benefit from my existence more than detract from it. I have tried and will continue to try to do more good than harm.

I also try to teach my son positive values, how to be a good person and do my best to raise him with the skills that he will need to be a successful, contributing member of society.

Rounding out this chapter on shortcuts and vices, know that there are temptations to happiness around every corner. If it's easy and especially tempting, it's probably not going to lead to anything fulfilling.

You are bound to make mistakes and bad choices as you go through life. When you do, try and fix them as soon as you can.

For all mistakes, even those you cannot change, take personal accountability, look inwards and learn from them.

Gain a new perspective. If you do this, your chances of repeating them have been greatly reduced.

SECTION 4: 36 RULES TO A FULFILLING LIFE

There is generally no logic to the order of these rules as they are not meant to be followed in any order. While I do feel that some are more important than others, that is my version of a life fulfilled.

You will find your own definition of what makes you feel most fulfilled. This will come to you as you travel down your own path.

Even though our exact definitions on a fulfilling life may be different and our emphasis on one rule over another may be greater or lesser, the rules are still the same for everyone.

As I list the rules, I try and give examples and explanations in an easy to read, light and entertaining way. I will often tell personal stories and experiences, or stories that I have heard throughout my life. I will cite pop culture, various statistics and historical events.

In most cases, I will also give you a few specific steps included to help follow a rule. In other cases, there are already libraries of information, many with various tactics, already written on how to follow one specific rule or another. Those are typically the rules most people have the hardest time with.

My purpose in laying out the 36 rules to a fulfilling life, is to help you understand what they are and why they are all so important.

What works for you in getting a rule to stick as a part of your lifestyle may not be the same thing that works for another.

This book is not all-encompassing. If it were, it would be thousands of pages long and filled with a lot of irrelevant information to many people.

It would also be a magic bullet and remember, anyone selling you a magic bullet is a charlatan.

This is a guide and like any other guide, you need to put it into practice to make it work. You may also need further, more detailed assistance or consultation in specific areas.

RULE 1: DO NOT CHASE HAPPINESS - CHASE FULFILLMENT!

There is nothing wrong with wanting to be happy. I think you should savor every moment of happiness as if it were your last. Just don't chase after it.

While I have mentioned this several times throughout this book, even in the title, I really need this to sink in.

Happiness does not last forever! Happiness does not bring you peace or shield you from sadness.

Happiness does not intrinsically lead to fulfillment because chasing happiness all the time is inherently selfish. You will never meet a selfish person with a truly fulfilled life, no matter how rich, successful or happy they may appear.

There are many paths that you can take while chasing happiness. Paths that can harm you and those around you. They can cause permanent damage physically, emotionally and spiritually. Chasing happiness has selfishly ended many lives far too soon.

The path to fulfillment, on the other hand, is a quest you can and should take your entire life. The more fulfilled your life is, the more of those happy stops you will have along your journey.

There is still a possibility that your quest for fulfillment may lead you to danger, even death in some cases. This greatly depends upon what your purpose in life is.

There is one major difference that should be noted, between death or danger while chasing happiness and death or danger on your path to fulfillment.

When your time comes, hopefully many, many years from now and you are lying on your deathbed, knowing that you have done all that you could, to live a life fulfilled will bring you peace and comfort.

It will also give your loved one's peace and comfort as they will see you as someone who lived with a purpose, a life lived with true meaning.

RULE 2: HAVE A PURPOSE AND RECOGNIZE THIS PURPOSE MAY CHANGE THROUGHOUT YOUR LIFE!

This might be one of the most important and most challenging of the 36 rules to a fulfilling life.

The sooner you find your purpose and start working towards it, the more fulfilled you will be.

If there comes a point in life where your purpose must change, the sooner you realize this as an inevitability, the sooner you will find your new purpose and return towards the path to fulfillment.

When speaking about having a purpose, this does not have to be your job or career.

The world is a dynamic place with many moving cogs and wheels. Sure, there are more important and higher paying cogs and wheels than others but nevertheless, they must all be filled by someone, or the machine of society will break down.

There are tons of jobs out there that are far from glamorous but still need to be filled by someone. Chances are, many of them do not feel as fulfilling as you would like them to be.

Hell, there is even a whole TV show dedicated to them called, "Dirty Jobs", hosted by Mike Rowe. Even if you hold one of these so-called, "Dirty Jobs", take pride in what you do.

It is very rare for one's true purpose in life to be how you earn a living. If you can turn your purpose into your career or vice versa, you are one of the fortunate few.

"Do what you love and you will never work a day in your life" is terrible career advice for most people. There are tons of jobs out there that pay a good salary, are in high demand, that also give you the resources and time to pursue your true purpose, spend time with your loved ones and do whatever you want with the rest of your life.

Do you think most Attorneys love lawyering? Did you know the JD "Juris Doctorate" is the least used, advanced degree people obtain?

Most don't get this degree because the law is their passion, their purpose. All but the very few get the degree because it affords them the opportunity (i.e. money), in many cases to pursue their purpose in a variety of different careers (Or at least gives them the opportunity financially, if not career based).

With that said, there are many excellent attorneys that are great at what they do and feel it is their life's purpose. A lot of lawyers take on cases for free, "Pro bono" from time to time. These are generally cases that are fulfilling, help right a wrong and otherwise resonate with that specific Lawyer's true purpose.

The same thing goes for dentists. Do you think anyone ever says, "God, I just love sticking my face in other people's filthy mouths"? I'm not saying that dentists don't find their career choice fulfilling. They are doctors and help people every day.

The medical field is usually one that is a calling and true purpose for many. A lot of dentists even travel to 3rd world countries, just to help people who otherwise wouldn't receive it.

I'm sure dentistry is some people's true life's purpose. For others, it's just an excellent paying career that affords them with a lot of time off. Time off and money to pursue what they are passionate about.

Ironically, no matter what your career of choice is or how perfect most of your days are, how fulfilled you feel after a long day, there will always be times when it still feels like work, when you'd rather be doing something else. This is true even when your career is your life's purpose.

Many people spend their entire lives in search of their purpose. Most of these people have just been looking for what makes them happy. They have been fooling themselves into thinking that what makes them happy, must be their purpose.

We spoke before about how many people confuse fulfillment and happiness and how chasing happiness is futile, mainly because what makes a person happy can change with the wind.

Many people work to achieve a position or promotion because they believe it will make them happy and in turn, fulfill the purpose in life they seek. When they attain it, they feel a burst of happiness immediately after but are eventually let down. It was not their purpose.

They then try to find their purpose with a different job or entirely different career.

If this is you, try changing your perspective. If you wanted that job so bad or worked so hard to get it, it can't be that horrible. Plus, if this position affords you with the resources that you need to live a lifestyle you are comfortable with, it will likely give you the tools needed to find your purpose, outside of work.

While our purpose is usually hiding right under our noses, many people still never see it, never smell it, never find it. This is due to a paradox.

While finding your life's purpose leads to fulfillment, only seeking true fulfillment will lead to discovering your life's purpose. Therefore, there are 36 rules to fulfillment, not just one.

RULE 3: MAINTAIN A REAL-LIFE CONNECTION WITH THE PEOPLE YOU CARE ABOUT!

It started out as a joke, a group of teenagers all sitting around a table, in someone's house or coffee shop, all staring down at their phones and none of them talking with each other. A completely silent room was full of teenagers.

Could anyone before 1990 ever imagine this? The thing is, they were communicating with each other. Just not in the way anyone from the past could have ever imagined.

These teenagers were text messaging each other. The modern version of passing written notes back and forth during school. Except no one was in class and there were no adults in the room, forcing them to be quiet.

What was once a last resource or communication, when talking out loud wasn't an option, has become the preferred method of conversation. Even when in the same room for many people.

Technology evolves and texting can be damn convenient sometimes. Maybe you have something quick to say, maybe you need to communicate but any other form would be prohibitive or disruptive.

Maybe you're just too tired or lazy at the moment and don't feel like getting into a full-on, drawn-out conversation now. All of those are acceptable reasons to use text and other instant messaging applications.

Texting or instant messaging just shouldn't replace real-life communication, using your voice. Talking is a skill and a very important one at that. Muscles will atrophy while not being used, like when recovering in a hospital bed or floating through space.

Your verbal skills will atrophy in the same way if you don't use them. It's the same principle behind someone who once spoke a second or third language fluently. If you don't keep doing it regularly, you might remember the basics but your fluency will be lost.

People probably said disparaging things about the telephone when it first came out. I'm sure this isn't unique to text messaging. However, the telephone should still not replace in-person conversation and connection. The telephone and text do not allow you to pick up on body language or other physical, emotional cues.

The telephone is better than text because you can at least here an emotional inflection in another person's voice. We try and utilize emojis and acronyms to get across our emotional inflection through text but it doesn't always translate the way we intend it to. Many times, to embarrassingly, inappropriate hilarity.

Even using video chat services like Skype or Facetime are not perfect. They're better. Now you can pick up on the inflection of a person's voice and even see their body language but you still lack the ability to physically touch the person you are communicating with.

Sometimes that may be a plus, especially in the #MeToo era, though many times, it's a minus. Most often, what is needed can only be achieved with a real life, in-person interaction. It is always the most fulfilling.

Use technology to help maintain a connection, especially with those who may be separated by long physical distances. It is a tool that can be and should be used to help us live a fulfilling life. As useful a tool as it is, it will never be able to replace a real-life connection in the world as we know it.

As technology advances and VR, AR and AI become more and more advanced, I can see a future where a user can simulate conversations with relatives who have long passed away. Will that not be an amazing tool with the potential to help one gain closure from a loss? Abso-freakin-lutely!

I'm also sure someone, at some point, will be writing about how unhealthy it is. How it is being used to hang onto the figment, cyber-based version of a person's being... How unethical and immoral it is.

I'm no fortune teller and we'll just have to wait and see what happens. For now, if you want a fulfilling life, maintain a real-life connection with the people you care about, while you still can.

*Text messaging can also be a great method of defusing conflict within a relationship, especially if children are in the house. It protects them from hearing anything and forces you to think as you type, rather than saying insulting words out of impulse.

RULE 4: GET INVOLVED WITH YOUR COMMUNITY TO MAKE A POSITIVE IMPACT - NOT FOR SOCIAL CAPITAL!

The caveat at the end is of most importance when using this rule to create a fulfilling life. Becoming involved within your community and neighborhood, volunteering or just trying to help when and where you can, is always a positive thing.

So... Even if you do not follow the last part of the rule, you will typically do more good than harm, which is another rule in and of itself.

This book isn't just about doing more good than harm, it's about living by all 36 rules to have a truly fulfilling life.

When you do good things without expecting anything in return, not even kudos, it always feels better and is always more fulfilling.

One reason for this is because people in general, tend to overvalue the work they do. If doing that work for an unspecified expectation, of something in return, it will most likely always be less than you were expecting (Even that pat on the back).

Another reason the last part of this rule is so important is that social gatherings can be a hotbed for gossip. If you are the type of person that likes to gossip, stop doing this immediately.

Do not get involved with your community just to hear the juicy gossip on what's happening with whom.

That will do nothing to make your life more fulfilled. It will most certainly earn you a reputation as someone with loose lips, someone who cannot be trusted. Especially if it is you that is spilling the beans on all the salacious, neighborhood scandals.

When you volunteer your time, your words of encouragement and your help, without expecting anything in return, it always feels good.

Not in a self-important way, or self-aggrandizing way, if you feel either of those things, you should do a little soul searching. It also shouldn't make you feel like a better person than those who didn't help. Just feel good for what you have done to make society a little better place to live in.

It really doesn't even have to be within your own neighborhood or immediate community, but they are great places to start. Typically, there are never enough resources available in those areas and your assistance is almost always useful and appreciated.

The other main benefit of getting involved in your community is the social aspect. It can be a great way to meet new friends and form meaningful relationships with people who live near you. I stress meaningful relationships because not all relationships are meaningful. Some can be very toxic.

Please don't be the toxic one who joins in to, "Help" your community. That is pretty much the only way to turn this rule into a negative, doing more harm than good.

When I was a child, my father was in the fire service. One year, he and my mother got involved to help run the local Toys for Tots, or similar charity.

It was specifically to help give children in local community living facilities (I don't know if you can call them orphanages anymore) a little magic around Christmas. Something every child deserves to feel, whether around the holidays or not, religious or non-religious. I was probably 7 or 8 years old when he pulled into our driveway in a huge dump truck.

This was not just any ordinary dump truck. It was a dump truck filled with presents and toys, mainly wrapped in colorful paper or at minimum, lots of ribbon if oddly shaped. He told me to jump in the passenger seat and proceeded to take me with him all over town.

We got the honor of playing Santa Claus and Santa's helper, though not in any costumes, to disenfranchised, misfortunate and abused children, some without any families, all over what would one day be known as Silicon Valley.

As special as that whole day was for me, there was one moment that still stands out so much that I can feel it in my heart like it was yesterday.

We were in a children's facility and there was a boy, older than I, maybe around 10. There was also a giant stuffed bear. Now me, being a tough 7 or 8-year-old was no longer into stuffed animals. I liked toy guns, swords, dinosaurs, baseball and action figures.

The moment this older boy saw this giant stuffed bear, his eyes lit up with excitement. He immediately ran to it, giving it the biggest bear hug

I had ever seen. I then noticed tears running down his face, tears of joy knowing that his new stuffed friend would bring him comfort.

Even now, 30 years later, my eyes still well up when thinking about his reaction. That was the greatest lesson my parents ever taught me on the gift of giving. Of getting involved within your community to make a positive impact, without expecting anything in return.

In doing so, I received more than anything I could have ever imagined. I still get involved at some capacity every year, even if it's just buying a bunch of toys and donating them.

This is a lesson that I will teach my son. Not in the same way, as I don't see myself having that same opportunity. However, in a couple of years, if not sooner, we will be making a trip to the local Children's Hospital and bringing them a car full of toys and making a new, annual tradition.

If you have children, I highly recommend doing this. Many of the kids there are facing serious illness and pain that no one should have to go through.

Even if you can just bring in one new toy, you will help make a special kid smile when smiling was the last thing on their mind. You will also be teaching your own children important lessons that will last a lifetime.

That's called a double win!

RULE 5: BE KIND TO OTHERS!

This is something we all learn in preschool, if not well before. I'm certainly not about to offer you some groundbreakingly profound piece of advice.

However, it is something that we all need to be reminded of from time to time. It is a quintessential element of a life fulfilled, yet one that appears, at least on the surface to be lacking more now, than ever before.

Have we forgotten how to be kind to others? Especially those we don't really know or personally care for? What about those we say we care about the most? What about those we don't always agree with?

Over the past few years, more marriages have fallen apart, friendships lost and families strained simply because they do not agree with each other's choice in political affairs.

This should terrify you and is doing more to divide our country, our society, and the world than any politician could ever do. They can't seem to get anything done! Even when they try their hardest!

It's easiest however to blame Washington, to blame politics. No offense if you're a politician! If you are, do me a favor here and there and I'll be happy to add something special for you in my next book (wink, wink).

It's much harder to blame ourselves. XYZ politician is not personally calling you and ordering you to stop being friends, family or married to one person or another. Not yet at least. Not if we have a free society.

Only we have the power to take that away from ourselves. You are making the decision, on your own accord, if you end a relationship based upon politics.

Maybe if you both made the decision to just be kind to each other, to respectfully hear each other out, agree to disagree or just not talk about contentious topics, you would still have a relationship that is more fulfilling than not. A heart filled with more joy than hate.

(Newsflash! Many politicians on both sides of the aisle are good friends in real life. When they aren't pretending to be angry at each other, in front of the cameras, for your votes.)

You can still see kindness every day in many places. I still hold the philosophy that most people are generally more good than bad. That most people will typically do the right thing when given the opportunity.

I still believe in our collective culture and that we can find a way back to solidarity. We must first though, remember this basic rule; to be kind to each other.

If we can't do that, our world will end faster than climate change will ever have a chance to do, on its own or human-aided.

(Side note: If this book could get even a fraction of the coverage climate change does, it would be a New York Times bestseller within a week. Help me out here! Can't a straight, white male ever get a break? ;)

I spoke a lot about the cancer of, "Me! Culture. " How we have been taught, as adults to protect our own self-interests over the interests of everyone else. Sometimes at any cost. How this is aiding to a population incredibly unfulfilled and a society in decline.

I also talked about the 8 primary human emotions, disgust is one of them. I spoke of how since disgust must be learned, it can be unlearned.

We need to do the same thing here. We must unlearn the "Me! Culture" by first de-glamorizing the "Me! Culture." Then we can get back to basics.

This shouldn't be too hard for parents of small children. Nearly all day, every day, we teach them to share and play nice with others. It's time we start taking some of our own advice. It's the foundation of civilization, of society and the bedrock of a fulfilling life.

Start with what I like to call, "Kind light". Conscientiously hold open doors for strangers, smile more, offer up your seat on public transit (or at least pick up your bag from the seat next to you), let people merge in traffic, you know, simple things like this.

One thing I noticed from one part of the country to another is that in one part, people tend to literally and unabashedly rush to beat someone to the front of the line. Almost always with a scowl on their face or another look of displeasure, like they were breathing in bad air. Then while standing there, maybe a foot away, would do everything they could to avoid eye contact, knowing what they just did was rude.

That feeling by the way, is called shame but that feeling still doesn't stop them from doing it again and again. It's all about me baby!

In other parts of the country, people will walk at their normal pace while on the way to a line. If you happen to get there at the same time, a funny moment of almost friendly conflict breaks out, telling the other person to go first.

This generally only lasts a second or two until one person accepts, says thank you and they both feel good about what just occurred. They may even strike up a little friendly banter about this or that while waiting for the checker.

Small things like this go a long way towards feeling happier, making a bad day better, a little bit nicer and feeling more fulfilled.

RULE 6: TRY NOT TO BE A JERK! WHEN YOU ARE A JERK, RECOGNIZE THIS AND APOLOGIZE!

Sometimes you might have to deal with someone that makes it hard to show genuine kindness at a certain time, especially if they are being rude or otherwise insulting to you.

Everyone has bad days from time to time and not everyone knows how to deal with unpleasantries (put nicely) in a healthy way. In this case, at least try not to be a jerk in return. If all else fails and you stoop to their level... or lower, recognize your jerkiness as soon as possible and apologize.

This goes back to another preschool rule about two wrongs not making a right. In the situation described above, be the bigger person and go first.

Saying, "I'm sorry" was never the easiest thing to do but for some reason, the older you get, the harder it gets to apologize. Maybe this has something to do with having to admit that you were at least partially wrong.

Now let's say you were having a really bad day. You just your job, your wife is divorcing you and just as you were leaving for work that morning, found your dog had keeled over and died.

For all intents and purposes, that's a pretty shitty day. Now to top it off, you're driving home, just wanting to crawl into bed and hopefully find a little solace hiding under your blankets.

You're stopped at a traffic light and BAM! Someone rear ends you. Luckily there are no injuries and it wasn't at high speed, but now the shiny red bumper on your brand-new car is dented and scratched up.

How easy would it be to funnel all your loss, sadness and rage from everything that happened earlier in the day, to that relatively innocent person who hit you? A person who made a simple driving error, just like you could have done any other day.

What if I told you the person that hit you had just gone through everything you did that same day. Not only that, before they left their office for the last time, hung up the phone with their Doctor, being diagnosed with a terminal illness?

Would you still want to take your anger out on them? Especially now that they're also about to lose their health insurance and could very well die? Or might you show them a little empathy? At least recognize the fact that the fender bender isn't a big deal and can be easily fixed.

My point is that you never really know what someone else has going on in their lives. There is usually a reason, aside from just being an asshole that someone intentionally acts unfriendly to you. With that said, there are genuine assholes in the world. Do your best to have empathy or just ignore them.

We all go through stressful events or moments throughout our days, where being kind to others is difficult at best. When this happens, at least try not to be a jerk!

When you are a jerk, recognize this and apologize! You will feel better, the other person will feel better and in turn, that's one more step down the path to a fulfilling life.

RULE 7: BE RESPECTFUL DURING CONFLICTS WITH OTHERS!

Are you starting to see a pattern here? At least with these last few rules? No matter how kind we are or how much effort we put into not being a jerk, we are bound to have conflict from time to time.

Conflict in and of itself is not a bad thing. It's not the same as a fight or argument. Those are conflicts taken to a higher level. In other words, all arguments and fights start out as a conflict but not every conflict escalates to an argument or fight.

A conflict is simply a disagreement between two or more parties. We all have our own brains, our own experiences to draw from and in many cases, different amounts or accuracy of information. This is a natural recipe for the occasional conflict.

It is how we deal with this conflict that determines whether the outcome is healthy or not. Whether this conflict leads us down the path to fulfillment or off a thorny side trail.

I am not a Marriage Counselor but I'd be willing to bet, most couples that seek out marriage counseling do so to find healthy ways of dealing with their conflicts. To fix the breakdown in communication that has lead from a natural, healthy conflict, to a wrecking ball of matrimonial destruction.

I'd also be willing to bet that in many cases of infidelity, this is at least partially the cause. It is a breakdown in communication, stemming from the inability or unwillingness to deal with conflict in a healthy way.

Sometimes there are clear issues of abuse. In those cases, your best option is to find a way to safety as quickly and as quietly as possible. You will then want to speak with your local law enforcement authorities and develop a plan to collect evidence, retrieve your belongings, and make a plan to stay safe. Therapy is probably also a petty smart next step.

When dealing with conflict, be respectful to one another. Do not yell or raise your voice. Do not purposefully say hurtful things. If you do, apologize immediately. Stick to the issue of contention and have a healthy debate.

In most cases, a fair compromise can be made. In other cases, one party may have just needed more information to share your same perspective. In other cases, simply agree to disagree.

In cases where you agree to disagree, it depends upon the relationship you have with this person and your current dealings when determining where to go next. If it's a business transaction that you can't find a middle ground on, part ways amicably.

Follow the old saying about not burning bridges. Just because you couldn't strike a deal this time doesn't mean you won't be able to at some other point, in some other transaction, a little further down the road.

If you are a person known for showing respect, even in times of conflict, the likelihood of this happening increases exponentially. You become known as someone respectful and enjoyable to do business with.

This helps with all your relationships and good relationships are a pillar in leading a fulfilling life.

RULE 8: BELIEVE IN SOMETHING GREATER THAN YOURSELF!

When taken at face value, this is probably the most controversial rule in my entire book. Though it doesn't have to be. Please allow me to explain.

Although it may sound this way, I'm not saying you must subscribe to some form of organized religion to live a fulfilling life. That you must believe in a deity, a divine creator of man, animal, plant, and universe.

That you must subscribe to their doctrine, gospel, all their teachings and stories, however far-fetched or implausible under the laws of physics as we know them.

As I mentioned in the preface, I myself do not subscribe to any one organized religion, although baptized Catholic as a baby. This was not my choice, as it is not for most people brought up to believe in organized religion.

That is generally the way of religion. We are often taught or forced to believe, by our parents or other family members - never questioning our faith. This is how religion is primarily spread.

I went through a phase as a staunch Atheist. During this phase, I probably learned more about religion, in many of its forms than the most religious zealots.

I read books, written by man, supposedly the word of God, Allah, Shiva, Vishnu, Jesus Christ and so on and so forth. There are many good lessons to be learned in all of them. I will never discount them of that.

They all also had one thing in common; they were books written by man, generally many decades, if not hundreds of years after the last living witness, whose word was being written about had gone.

Even the word of Buddha, a religious, middle of the road, independent thinker, was not written down until 400 years after his passing. His teachings were spread by word of mouth, much like most every other religion in the history of mankind. However saintly you believe the transcribers to be, they were only men, just as fallible as you or me.

I have also read books by respected and staunch secularists such as Richard Dawkins. He has made many strong arguments against theism, especially in his book, "The God Delusion". In it, his basic premise is that to believe in organized religion and a personal, supernatural creator, one must be delusional. He goes on to give justification in support of his beliefs throughout the entire book.

It was and still is very hard for me to argue with some of his statements against the absence of a personal, supernatural creator. I also subscribe to his belief that you must not have to believe in religion to be of good moral character.

Though as strong as his arguments are, they also never lead me to clear, irrefutable evidence of the absence of a creator. A certain, "God" if you will, of some kind.

I do not believe that by choosing to believe in religion or a personal, supernatural creator that you must be delusional. There are too many negative connotations and absolute lack of evidence to the contrary to associate faith with delusion.

If your faith does not interfere negatively with the lives of others, others who may hold different beliefs than your own, I only see it as a positive step down the path to a fulfilling life.

There are over 4,200 recognized religions in the world and guess what, they all think theirs is the only path to righteousness.

Tolerance is of most importance when speaking to religion. I think religion in general is a good thing. I like living in religious neighborhoods and have many religious friends. Friends that understand the spirit of what is being taught and are tolerant of those with different beliefs. They tend to be good people of good character.

Fundamentalism is the enemy of tolerance. That is when religion goes from more good than bad to more harm than good.

When the "Word of God", written by man is taken so literally, to the letter, without regard to metaphor or changing times, without question, that they will harm or kill others in defense or offense of those beliefs, those beliefs have become delusional and destructive.

If you take these ancient words so literally that you create laws to oppress others, in the name of them, you have also grown delusional and destructive. Destructive to yourself, your family, your neighbors and civilization.

With this being said, I do believe that to have a fulfilling life, you must believe in something greater than yourself. There are times in everyone's life when you need hope. When you cannot find the solution, you are looking for on your own. It is during these times that you must at least look to the universe if you do not subscribe to organized religion.

Open your mind to the possibility of an unconscious solution. An unexpected idea from your own mind, a new experience, coincidental lesson or the opportune wisdom of someone else, maybe someone completely random.

Also, know that you are not the first person to go through what you are going through and you will most certainly not be the last.

Do you need something more, "Tangible" than faith in religion or a spiritual connection to the universe? If you intend to follow the 36 rules to a fulfilling life, you must still believe in something greater than yourself.

Here's an easy one and ironically one of the things that make organized religion so appealing: Community! Organized religions provide their members with a close sense of community and connection to each other. That is one of the greatest benefits of a church congregation. Congregation being the opportune word.

As you know already, getting involved in your community happens to be rule number 4 and you don't have to be involved with any religious activities to join in. By getting involved with your neighbors and being a part of your community, you are also becoming a part of something bigger than yourself.

You can't deny that a community of people is bigger than yourself. Therefore, you are automatically believing in something bigger than yourself and following the eighth rule.

RULE 9: CONTINUE TO LEARN AND GROW THROUGHOUT YOUR ENTIRE LIFE!

I remember an old TV episode of "Married with Children" where one of the shows cast members, a sexy, dim-witted blonde teen/twenty-something named Kelly Bundy was featured on a game show.

She was tutored by her brother Bud, a smart, dorky, teenage boy, who thought he was cool but was completely self-unaware.

He could teach her semi-complex ideas such as the definition of a synapse. However, he ran into a small problem and described this to his father Al, "You see, if you took a gallon of knowledge and poured it into a shot glass of a brain, you're gonna spill some".

Every time he inserted a new idea, a new piece of knowledge into her brain, she lost some other form of basic information.

Now, this was done to comedic effect and I have a hard time seeing this show ever greenlit in the politically correct world of today. With that being said, this episode speaks to how fortunate we are to be able to learn as many new things as we are willing, throughout our whole lives.

As cliché as it is, "You learn something new every day" should be your motto. It's also easier than ever since most of us hold a computer in our pockets that will literally tell you anything about everything, whenever you want to know it.

This kind of screws those of us who longed to be able to bullshit our grandchildren one-day, spewing nonsense as fact, grand purveyors of knowledge on every topic.

As a glass half full kind of a guy, I think we still can. We'll just have to start when they're a little younger.

There is so much to learn about our universe, our world, our existence that has already been discovered and published in a litany of sources.

I'm certain this is just a small fraction of the new discoveries that will be made, as time progresses and new discoveries are built off each new discovery.

A curious mind is a healthy mind and you can't have a fulfilled life without a healthy mind. Not only will learning new things help stave off boredom, but it also gives you something to look forward to each day.

Develop many different hobbies as you progress through life. They give you knowledge, make you more interesting to talk to and provide a multitude of experiences, some very exciting.

Do you want to be known one day as a wise old man or old woman, or the crazy old bat? Honestly a little of both would probably be more interesting, not to mention, realistic.

Studies also show that keeping your mind engaged is critical to the fending off degenerative brain disorders. So, there is also that to keep in mind. (No pun intended)

You don't have to be in school to learn and you are never too old to go back to school either. People worry about going back to school at a later age but there are some advantages.

Honestly, the older you get, the more likely you are to see through the bullshit bias and charisma of your professor, to the actual core of the lesson. You are also there solely to learn and expand your mind, not get wrapped up in groupthink (which shrinks your mind) and popularity contests.

In any case, this rule has nothing to do with higher education and everything to do with making the choice to continue to learn and educate yourself.

Make the commitment to keeping your mind open to new information as it's made available and not dismiss it simply because it runs contrary to what you learned in the past.

Always question the source of the information you are receiving and don't purposely seek out information from sources that confirm what you think you already know or what you want to hear.

You can and will find any number of studies. These studies will unequivocally and without question confirm and deny the exact opposite of each other.

You can often correctly guess the outcome of a study, just by knowing who is financing it. Be mindful of this. Review all opposing sources and know the truth of anything controversial, is likely somewhere in the middle.

RULE 10: GET OUT INTO NATURE AS MUCH AS POSSIBLE!

Just put on some clothes, (I really don't want to think of you sitting on a clean white chair, reading this butt-ass naked) strap on your shoes and walk out of the door.

If you're fortunate enough to where you can access a hiking trail within walking distance, thank your lucky stars. If you can't but you are in driving distance of some actual nature, drive there. Be it the mountains, a beach, the desert, a lake, a pond, anywhere that's not filled with a ton of people.

Once there, walk around. Take in the scenery and natural beauty while you breathe in some fresh air.

I can't even begin to emphasize how therapeutic this is, especially if you can also combine it with some form of exorcising.

If you do combine it with exercise, I must insert a caveat, let yourself get out of, "The zone" mentally from time to time, so you can fully appreciate your surroundings.

If you live in a big city or don't have a car, at least try to find a nice park you can walk around and enjoy.

Another caveat, if you are a middle-aged male walking by yourself, try your best not to look like a creep. Unless of course, you are a creep.

Then wear a sign that says you are, so you can be avoided/arrested. Or maybe you should just follow that restraining order and stay out of the park and its surrounding area.

In all seriousness, I hope you all have learned by now that even though I am writing a serious book, on a serious topic, it's alright to not always be serious. It's alright to laugh at things that might be inappropriate. Being uncomfortable can be one of the things that makes a joke funny in the first place.

I know this is a little off topic but I really feel it necessary in the society and culture of today to bring up. Joking doesn't make you a bad person and laughing at a joke doesn't make you a bad person. Being a bad person makes you a bad person and really, who are you to judge?

Another cliché that we've seem to have forgotten is that laughter is the best medicine.

There is a thing called a macabre sense of humor, that to an outsider might sound insensitive, dark and inappropriate.

These insensitive, inappropriate jokes have been proven to legitimately help people cope with incredibly difficult, graphic and painful situations most of you will be lucky enough to never witness.

Now back to your regularly scheduled programming. (Or reprogramming for some of you... just kidding!)

I really can't stress enough how getting out into nature will help you feel more fulfilled. You must do it!

I grew up with the foothills, trails, the ocean and mountains as a regular part of my life. Even still, the first time I went to Yosemite as a teenager, I will never forget just how small I felt.

We arrived in Yosemite Valley at night and I couldn't see what we were driving into. Especially as a passenger in the back of a friend's parent's van.

We had plans to do a 20 something mile backpacking trek from Tenaya Lake, over Clouds Rest, then down to a quick climb up the, "Safe" side of Half Dome and on back down to the valley, passing beside two impressive waterfalls.

As I mentioned, it was late when we arrived so I pretty much went straight to bed. I wanted to be rested for the following day's activities. When I woke up the next morning and looked up.... All around me... The grandiosity of the mountains, the majesty of this perfectly crafted speck on this planet.

It felt like I had been picked up and placed in the middle of the most beautiful painting I had ever seen. I completely understand how it captivated and inspired Ansel Adams and many others as it did.

The whole trip, I was continuously amazed each and every day. It was physically tough, my whole body ached as bad as it ever had, I remember nearly freezing one night as it rained and water dripped onto me through my makeshift shelter.

On night two, I woke up to a giant bear a few feet from my head as I slept next to the campfire.

The next day, as I was making my way down the trail, a rattlesnake jumped out of a hollow tree stump, striking out at me. If I hadn't instinctively jumped away from the rattling sound, he would have surely struck my leg. Altogether, it was one of the greatest experiences I have ever had.

I have been back several times and each time I go back, I am still awestruck by its beauty. It also gets a little more crowded every time, as most special places tend to do.

Luckily, there are still many spots in this world that offer similar experiences to become one with nature. If only for a few moments.

Make those moments happen often, while you still can and I promise, you will have a much more fulfilling life.

RULE 11: STAY ACTIVE!

As much as I love getting out into nature and as easy as it is for me to walk out of my door to do it, sometimes I still need a kick in the butt, from my wife.

I'm pretty sure I've already mentioned this a time or two but I work a regular, full-time job, besides writing. I also have a side business.

I've also mentioned that my wife works full time as well. We live a modern lifestyle which means that we split up household chores evenly (I do the things she hates and she does the things I hate). Did I mention we have a fair amount of property? That tends to keep me busy with some heavy duty, power tool, fix this, trim that kind of work.

Luckily my wife really enjoys gardening and knows what flowers to plant where, what time of year to plant them outside and how to keep them alive and blooming in our sunroom during the snowy, Colorado winter. Also, how much to water them (and not forget) because without her, they'd all die with my brown thumb. We would have nothing but cactus if it were all up to me. Even then, they'd only have a 50/50 shot at surviving.

We do all this while trying to spend as much time with our soon to be 5-year-old as we can. Reading to him, practicing numbers, math, playing catch, regular parent stuff to a near kindergartener.

He likes to, "Help" with whatever we're doing (Parents, you know what this really means) but it teaches him responsibility and teamwork, while also getting to hang out with us.

He's very outgoing and never lets us forget when he is around. Some might say he has a "Spirited" personality. He would also rather be outside running around than playing video games.

This is partially due to us hiking with him a few times a week, in a backpack carrier from when he was 6 months old. The rest is probably due to genetics. "I want to go on a nature walk" is one of his favorite things to say and do.

You can probably count a lot of what we do as "Staying active" but that's not really what I mean besides the yard work and gardening. Yard work totally counts! It's hard work.

I remember driving by my aunt and uncle's house one day a few years ago. My uncle was older, probably 80 at the time but was outside slamming a fence post into the ground with a sledgehammer.

He kept active in his yard and had plenty of interests. He was also fairly healthy right up until around the last 6 months of his life. I think that had a lot to do with him staying active for as long as he could

By staying active, I'm really talking about going to the gym, walking around your neighborhood, hiking, biking, skiing, ice skating... Stuff that gets your heart pumping, blood flowing or at least your legs moving. This keeps you physically healthy and you can't live a fulfilling life without your health.

You only have one body and should do your best to keep it healthy for as long as you can. I'm not talking about unrealistic, photoshopped magazine pictures but I'm also not talking about glorifying an unhealthy lifestyle, filled with poor food choices and laziness, in the name of, "Body positivity".

According to the CDC, the average American woman in 1960 weighed 140 pounds. As of 2015, that weight was up 18.5% to 166.2 pounds. By 2017 it went up to 170.5 pounds. In the 1960s, the average American man weighed in at 166.3 pounds while tipping the scales in 2015 at an average of 195.5 pounds. That also went up in just two years to 197.8 pounds. There is nothing healthy about these numbers and the upward trend.

I know we're all busy and it can be hard to find time to cook but a cultural attitude shift about accepting yourself, no matter what isn't helping. Especially because for the first time in history (for a variety of reasons), our average life expectancy is lowering.

Type 2 diabetes, which used to be called, "Adult-onset diabetes" is now prevalent in children under 10 years old. In my opinion, that is tantamount to child abuse. There is no amount of positive body image talk that can make this healthy.

Accepting the things about yourself that you cannot change is what body positivity should really be about. Trying to talk yourself into the "Big is beautiful" movement when it's a blatant excuse for making unhealthy choices is not only stupid, it's dangerous.

Again, you don't have to be rail thin and there is no such thing as the perfect body, there are legitimately big boned people, just be healthy.

Fooling yourself into thinking you are happy living an unhealthy lifestyle, that you have complete control over, is not fulfilling in any way. You don't have to be a fitness model or spend hours a day in the gym. Just try and be relatively healthy.

I'm sorry if I'm offending anyone reading this right now. That is surely not my intention. Please remember, this book is not about how to accept yourself while living a mediocre life. This book lays out the 36 rules to a truly fulfilling life. Sometimes the truth hurts.

I'll say it one more time, you can't live a truly fulfilling life without staying active and you can't stay active if you are morbidly obese. I of all people can empathize with you.

Even though I know this to my core, have no mobility issues and have lived a very active lifestyle, sometimes I need a kick in the butt to not be lazy.

The last thing I need is someone empowering me to lay down on my sectional a little more, while watching TV and eating chips with nacho cheese sauce because, "I'm beautiful just the way I am".

Having someone to motivate you always helps. It sucks to get up off the couch when you're relaxed and comfortable. However, once you're out there, doing whatever activity you are doing, it feels even better.

Once you get that endorphin kick, you're glad you got up. It also feels good to know that you are doing something good for your body, as well as your mind.

RULE 12: TRAVEL AS OFTEN AS YOU CAN!

We talked about world travel as a positive way to decrease racism and biases. It's also something that makes you appreciate your country, in my case, The United States more than ever.

Unless you are blind, it truly opens your eyes to a lot of the things we take for granted every single day.

Whenever I hear someone say how terrible this country is, for whatever reason, I immediately know they have never traveled anywhere outside of the United States. If they have, they probably never left their resort or the developed world.

I am proud to be an American. It's a great place to live and I understand wholeheartedly why so many people from around the world want to live here.

With that said, I love to travel. I have traveled extensively and for long periods of time, even residing in foreign lands for some time. I rode a motorcycle around South America exploring villages, cloud forests and coastal highways.

I remember riding through what appeared to be a ghost town in Ecuador. Buildings all around on both sides of the road, a foggy mist lingering in the air as I rode slowly passed an old cemetery, with not a soul in sight.

That is until I came up upon a herd of bulls walking together, down the center of the road. I thought about turning around as the road seemed nearly impassable.

The town was kind of creeping me out as well, to be honest. Then I saw a gap between the bulls and decided to keep going. As I made my way through them, they started getting closer together, until my handlebars where mere inches from their horns.

It was as if they were trying to tell me to stop, turn around and go back the way I came. I pressed on and finally made my way to the front, then kept riding.

As I reached the other side of town, I learned why I hadn't seen anyone before. There was a giant festival at the other edge of town and everyone, literally everyone was there. It was an amazing experience to see and had I turned around, I would have had a completely different perspective of that day and of that town.

I also remember stopping at a restaurant in the middle of nowhere one day. It was just someone's house but they served food to passers-by on tables out front to earn money.

The floor was made of dirt, the house made of mud stucco-like material with rebar poking through the top of a corrugated metal roof, a pig walked around freely and a little girl sat at a small desk working on a typewriter, an actual typewriter.

It wasn't the best food I'd ever had, the restroom was filthy and the kitchen, questionable at best. It is, however, one of the most memorable restaurants I have ever eaten at.

It is not even that expensive to be a world traveler anymore. I've seen some discount travel packages, including air and hotel for several nights, that cost less than a weekend getaway or camping trip. I'm not joking!

However, if you have a fear of leaving the country or flying that you can't face (Even though you should), at least travel around your state and drive around the country.

There are a ton of things to be seen right here in The United States of America. Things that will also open your mind and your eyes more than you could even think possible.

I don't remember where I heard this quote about travel but I didn't make it up. I have to share because it sums up the experience to me and answers the question of why: "We travel not to escape life, but for life not to escape us."

Now maybe I'm just a simpleton but I've found this statement to be profoundly accurate. It also explains why it's impossible to live a fulfilling life without travel.

So please, make time. I know it's hard to do, especially with full-time jobs and families but it can be done. The late Warren Miller, an amazing storyteller, and pioneer of the ski film industry always said, "If you don't do it this year, you'll be one year older when you do." -Warren Miller.

Truer words have never been spoken.

RULE 13: CREATE GOALS / PLANS FOR YOUR FUTURE!

Just about every self-improvement book, article, seminar or website tells you to set goals and plans for your future. They might say it in different ways or give you different opinions on what the most effective way to do it is.

Vision boards are pretty, "In" right now. I've also heard of superstitions like writing your main goal for the year on a piece of paper, lighting it on fire and drinking it in your champagne at the stroke of midnight, on New Year's Eve. Many people use a combination of different methods.

The truth is, the most effective way of setting a goal is the one that makes you think of it often, which helps you stick to it. That's one of the things people like about vision boards or goals written on scratch pads and calendars. You are almost forced to look at them, which keeps your goals at the top of your mind.

One thing you may not hear often is the further out you are planning, the more unrealistic your goal should appear to your current situation.

Now don't go crazy and imagine yourself King or Queen of the world. I don't mean that unrealistic. I mean to imagine yourself living your ideal life, whatever that may be. The reason being is this: Even if you miss your target, you're still going to be way closer to it than had you been, "A little more realistic".

The main caveat is that the closer your timeframe to this goal, say within a year, the more realistic it should be. Still set the bar high, just not quite as high as your long-term plans.

Every year, aim to make them a little better and a little higher. Let the universe know what you want and hold yourself accountable for making it happen. By this I mean to keep your eyes open and look for opportunities everywhere.

You never know where you might find an idea that will take you one step closer to reality. When you find that opportunity, do the work and make the most of it.

Contrary to some advice you may read, your dreams aren't just going to fall into your lap, without doing any work.

Also know that as the years go by, the things you once found very important, may not seem as important to you anymore. Therefore, you will have to readjust as you go. Even/especially you're big, crazy, long-term ones.

Think of your goals like roadmaps, without them, you might end up driving in circles or getting lost in a bad neighborhood. Also like maps, even if you have one, it may still take you longer to reach your destination than you initially thought.

A lot can happen as you drive down the road of life, on your path to fulfillment. Which leads me to rule number 14: Know that things will rarely go according to plan and learn to accept this.

RULE 14: KNOW THAT THINGS WILL RARELY GO ACCORDING TO PLAN BUT YOU MUST PERSEVERE!

History is riddled with instances of failure followed by success. In many cases, especially with some of the most successful people, the greatest ideas, the best inventions, they did not start out as planned and some form of failure was almost a requirement.

According to Forbes, 90% of startups fail. You can guarantee when this or that new business owner was drawing out their plan with excitement, failure was not at the front of their minds.

No one starts anything with the intention to fail. The fact of the matter is, most successful entrepreneurs had failed or nearly failed before they found out what worked. Something happened or wasn't considered and failure was imminent.

What separates successful entrepreneurs from those that are unsuccessful is the ability to learn from their mistakes, the ability to deviate from their plan when flaws become clear and... perseverance.

Sometimes deviating from your plan might be to completely close a business and reopen one in a whole different direction.

Sometimes it means learning to become a better manager and empower your talented employees rather than firing them over trivial differences in opinion.

Steve Jobs was ousted from Apple before returning in 1997 to help turn it into one of the world's most recognizable brands. Now we all know that Mr. Jobs was a perfectionist and there are plenty of stories about how difficult he was to work for.

That still doesn't change the fact that he was one of the greatest innovators and entrepreneurs of the last century.

He has been known for many great quotes, though one of my favorites, very apropos to this rule is this, "I'm convinced that about half of what separates successful entrepreneurs from nonsuccessful ones is pure perseverance." – Steve Jobs

You don't have to look very hard to find examples of perseverance paying dividends. Just turn on your TV. Think of all the beautiful people that move to Hollywood every year with plans to, "Make it big".

The clear majority of movie and TV stars didn't start out as household names. Most didn't know anyone in the business at all. The ones that became successful took tons of acting classes, developing their talent, their craft and went to audition after audition.

They faced rejection on a regular basis and it likely took them much longer to get their big break than they had anticipated. What separates the waiters from the movie and TV stars? Most of the time, pure perseverance.

Life is filled with ups and downs and things rarely go according to plan. Does that mean you shouldn't make plans? No, of course, you should. What it does mean is that you should also have a few backup plans at the ready, for when things go sideways.

You should also understand when to change direction and when to keep forging the same path. Sometimes you must trust in yourself over others. No one knows what is in your heart and in your head as well as you.

A lot of the time, the make or break it factor comes down to one thing, how bad you want it. If you want it that badly, you must persevere!

RULE 15: LEARN TO RESPECT/ACCEPT AUTHORITY!

This rule is based upon a complaint I had been hearing from numerous teacher friends of mine for at least the past 10 to 15 years.

Children and teenagers misbehaving in school is nothing new, however it has apparently been taken to a whole new extreme.

In some cases, students will blatantly defy their teachers and administrators from as early as elementary school through high school and beyond. They do this with no fear of repercussions or understanding of the potential consequences for their actions.

The consensus that I have heard regarding the heart of the problem, stems from parents not supporting the teachers. "My son/daughter is a good kid and would never do xyz behavior that you're speaking of".

Basically, parents are in denial that the problem may lie with their child and immediately jump to the conclusion that the teacher is wrong, that they are unfairly singling their child out due to personal vendetta or otherwise. This attitude of, "I can get away with anything" then follows the student into adulthood.

I started hearing similar concerns from employers regarding their younger employees. When asked to perform certain tasks, tasks that they felt were beneath them or, "Not in their job description", the younger employee would push back, without regard to the person making the request.

If you are a new person in a company, especially in a non-executive role and you are asked to make a pot of coffee or similar menial task, just do it. It has nothing to do with your gender in most cases and there is no pejorative meaning behind it.

If you are anyone other than the CEO and the CEO asks you to make a pot of coffee, just do it. I guarantee you that a successful VP would never take it personally if their CEO asked him/her to make a pot of coffee. They worked their way up to VP by being a team player and team players pitch in whenever and wherever needed.

This clearly just isn't about coffee, it's about anything that someone of greater authority may ask for. "Yes Sir" or "Yes Mam" are great words to learn and get used to saying. These are taught to say without thinking in the military and paramilitary organizations, like fire and police academies.

It's about learning to respect the authority and judgment of a person with greater experience. Will they always be right just because they have more experience? Of course not! No one is right all the time. The point is to give them the benefit of the doubt.

Unless of course, this has to do with an immediate safety issue. I was a reserve Firefighter and Paramedic and was told time and time again, "There is no such thing as rank when it comes to safety" and "We are all equal Safety Officers".

I think it's easy logic to understand in this case and I'm guessing that no matter what industry you work in, the same sentiment will ring true.

There is a pretty standard interview question in fire and police oral board interviews. "You are given an order from your direct superior officer while on an emergency scene and while on your way to complete that order, you are stopped by someone with an even higher rank and asked to perform a completely different task, what do you do?"

I include this example because it is not specific to public safety positions and should be answered in the same way without regard to your line of work.

The generally agreed upon, "Right" answer is to ask the higher-ranking officer to repeat/clarify his/her order if you have any questions regarding it. Then, respectfully inform them that you were just given another task by your direct supervisor.

Now, ensuring the higher-ranking officer has all the information you have, ask if he/she would still like you to immediately drop the first task you were given by your direct supervisor in favor of the task being assigned by him/her? In many cases, they will have you continue with your first order.

Other times, the higher-ranking Officers order will be of greater importance and they will have you drop the first order to complete theirs. In this case, the responsibility to communicate the change in assignment with your direct supervisor has been passed onto the higher-ranking officer, however, it is still a good idea to verify who will communicate this if the higher-ranking officer doesn't explicitly say they will do so. Someone will still be needed to complete your original task.

In non-emergency situations, in the business world, it might fall on you to do both assignments and use your judgment on what needs to be done first.

The one thing you should never do is dismiss the higher-ranking supervisor by telling them that you are already busy with something else. That is a clear disregard for their authority and will not do you any favors with career development.

If the person giving you the order or request is asking you to violate any laws, your personal morals and/or ethics, you must know and consider the consequences of your disobedience and be willing to accept them.

Never violate your morals and do not break the law just because someone of higher authority is asking you to. Their rank will never get you out of trouble with the law and you will have to live with yourself if you violate your morals.

This may be the case in an instance of quid pro quo sexual harassment. In this case, take notes (even after the fact) and write down as many specifics as possible including times and dates, take screenshots of text messages, basically, collect evidence. Then, you can either attempt to rectify the situation with your HR department if you have one/feel comfortable doing so, or consult with an attorney.

You should also know that as friendly as the people are in your HR department, they have one mission: To protect the best interest of the organization and save them from legal complications (Lawsuits).

If you approach your HR department first, never give them original copies of anything you may need down the road. If you are forced to, make sure you have backup copies.

Depending upon the company and how they react, you may need these documents if you must follow up with a lawsuit.

I am not an attorney but know that many of them will first ask how you tried to rectify the situation, before seeking legal action.

If you are in an encounter with a Law Enforcement officer, do what they say and follow their directions to the letter. Be as polite and respectful as possible, no matter how rude you think they are being.

Do not act fidgety and keep your hands out of your pockets, in clear view of the Officer. You will never win by arguing with a Police Officer.

If you believe you are innocent and are being unjustly persecuted for any number of reasons, the side of the road is not a courtroom.

Do not attempt to physically fight for your freedom. You don't want to force the Officer to become the Judge, Jury, and Executioner.

If the Police Officer wants to arrest you, follow their directions, go to jail and then plead your case to the judge with the help of an attorney.

You will never win by fighting with the Police and fighting with the Police will never help your case when you go in front of a judge.

The sooner you learn to respect and accept authority, the better your life will be. This should ideally start in childhood with learning to respect and accept the authority of a child's parents.

Many parents today are more concerned with becoming their child's friend than their parent.

You should bond with your child and do all sorts of fun things together. You should also make sure they respect your authority as their parental figures and obey what you tell them.

It is your responsibility to teach them morals, ethics and how to make reasonable decisions. You are not just responsible for their safety.

It is your responsibility to teach them to become positive, contributing members of society.

Sometimes, you are going to have to make them do things that they are uncomfortable with or that they would rather not do. Many parents tend to jump in too fast these days when their children face adversity.

I know you don't want to see them struggle but that struggle is what helps them build strength. You are not always going to be around to protect them and they will turn into adults at some point.

Give them the tools they need, teach them how to handle situations but let them practice themselves. Teach your child to fish or they will be living in your basement for the rest of their lives.

Also, know that children and teenagers are manipulative by nature. They need boundaries. They crave boundaries but they will always try and push those boundaries. They are trying to test you, to see what they can get away with.

Stay strong and continue to parent the best that you can. They will have plenty of friends throughout their lives but will only have two parents.

This is your most important job and they will appreciate you for it later.

RULE 16: LIVE IN THE MOMENT!

Some people make excuses, trying to outsmart themselves or others by saying that it's impossible to live in the moment while making plans/goals for the future.

A lot of addicts talk like this to avoid responsibility. They may not even be excuses; some people genuinely might not be able to see how this is possible.

On the contrary, I say. It is much easier to live in the moment if you know you have goals and a plan. It gives you the freedom to fully experience what is happening in the now. Much like having a budget, it is freeing.

Knowing how much money you have to comfortably spend on any given activity will ease your mind and let you think about what you are doing, not what is in your wallet and how you're going to pay the bill when it arrives.

With that said, some people can get a little too wrapped up in Rule 13, thinking only towards the future. That might be alright if we knew all our plans would always go off without a hitch, however, we already know the opposite to be true. Things will rarely go exactly according to plan.

Therefore, find the balance. Know what you are working towards but also experience life as it happens. This way, when the unanticipated does happen, it is that much easier to adapt.

It is true that there are some things in life that we must do, that we would rather skip over. That was the premise of the movie, "Click" with Adam Sandler. He was an architect that prioritized work over his family.
One evening, while shopping, he was given a powerful, magic remote to fast forward through parts of life that he didn't want to deal with.

He soon learned that those boring parts also contained valuable time and memories with the people he cared about. Before he knew it, he ended up old, divorced and had no real relationship with his children.

He was rich and successful in his career but all alone. He fast forwarded through everything that makes life matter. Lucky for him it was all a dream and he could go home with a different mindset.

That dream gave him the gift of perspective, now knowing how important it is to be present, in the moment, through all of life's ups and downs.

Up to this point, I have only spoken of those living in the future. If you're not going to live in the moment as much as you can, following a plan to reach an important goal is a worthy reason to put less emphasis on this rule.

Unfortunately, there are probably more people unable to enjoy the moment due to living in the past.

By living in the past, I'm not only talking about PTSD or being stuck in your glory days, I'm talking about all sorts of mental illness.

Depression and social/generalized anxiety, certain phobias and traumas of all sorts are great barriers to living in the moment.

These things typically stem from issues of the past that must be worked through with a professional. Reading this book alone will not teach you how to get to the root of each or any of these problems so that you can truly live in the moment.

We all know someone who has been affected by cancer, if not you yourself. There is a common theme running through every story of every person that sat in their doctor's chair and was given a countdown timer. How many days, weeks, months or years that they have left on this planet.

That must be one of the scariest feelings a person can go through. Nearly every single one of them said that after the initial shock, sadness, and stages of grief, it made them appreciate what little time they thought they had left.

It made them want to savor every moment they could with the people in their lives that they loved. It made them want to accomplish all the things they had been putting off due to fear or phobia.

Why must it take knowing you are about to die to make you truly want to live?

Another cliché that holds true is not appreciating what we have until we don't have it anymore. That may be a relationship, a house, a job or even your life.

All the fortunate souls who have beat their disease vow to never look at life the same again. Never take it for granted, live in and appreciate every single moment.

Even without a terminal diagnosis or freak accident (Which I know by experience, happens a lot more than you think), we have a finite time on this planet. Make the most of it, take your head out of the clouds or out from under your pillow and live in the moment.

Experience life in all its forms. Savor the bitter just as much as the sweet, sour and spicy.

Even if you do live a long and healthy life, and I pray that you do, how many special moments will you have? How many Christmas mornings will you get to see the excitement in the eyes of your children, waking up to see that, "Santa" paid them a visit? Maybe 6 or 7... at most, from when they are old enough to know the story and young enough to not know, "The truth".

That is not very many and those moments are truly magical, not to mention different each year.

You don't have to be Christian or even celebrate Christmas, with "Santa" at all, to understand the point I am trying to make. Many times, you won't even realize how special a moment truly was until it has passed.

There are many times in my life where I look back and think, why was I in such a rush to leave? Why didn't I ask a few more questions when I had the chance? Why didn't I stretch this moment out just a little longer?

When those moments happened to you, I hope you were fully there, fully in that moment. When they happen in the future, I hope you're not thinking about work or something inconsequential like that.

Live in the moment! How can you have a fulfilling life if you don't take the time to appreciate the one you have?

RULE 17: BE THANKFUL FOR THE LIFE YOU LIVE, THE PEOPLE THAT ARE IN IT AND THE THINGS YOU HAVE!

Do you want to know the secret to a completely unfulfilling life? It's quite simple and you don't need to follow 36 rules to do it: Take everything you have for granted and make yourself believe that you deserve, no, that you have the absolute right to much more of everything.

If you want to take it a step further and truly be miserable, blame someone or something else for whatever is lacking in your life.

No matter what's going on in your life, your living situation, your social situation, if you are reading this book, you likely have a lot to be thankful for.

I don't mean this in an egotistical way, about how you should be grateful for the wisdom I'm bestowing upon you (I hope you can feel my sarcasm).

For one, you know how to read, which means you have at least a basic level of education. You also have enough wisdom to realize you want to learn the tools needed to make the most of this life.

In addition, you have the means to either buy this book or borrow it from a friend. That gives you either expendable income or a social connection.

It's likely you have a pretty great life. I bet most of the people reading this book are on the upper end of the income scale, at least the middle class.

You probably own a home or at least have a roof over your head, a job (or working towards one), family, friends, food, a car (or two), hobbies, toys of all sorts. A lot of the time, people forget just how much they have going on for them in life.

Even the poor are doing better now than at any other time in history. Especially in the United States and the developed world. When I would go on emergency calls in poor neighborhoods, I would regularly see bigger and newer TVs in their apartments than I had myself, along with decent furniture, pictures and decorative art hanging around.

Those are just material things. Many of us have strong family relationships. Do we get along all the time? No. Do we have conflict, arguments and hold grudges? Yes, sometimes. Are they still your family and do you still love them? I think most us would say yes.

Family can be funny in that you don't have to like them to love them. Still, you should even be grateful for the ones you don't really care about. You know you have had some fond memories with them and will likely miss them when they're gone.

Maybe you don't have a big family or they have all passed away. You probably have some good times to look back on and be grateful for?

Maybe you never had the opportunity to know your family. You might have friends in your life that you look upon as family. Acquaintances that you enjoy spending time with.

Do you have your dream job? More than likely, the answer is no. Could things be better? Absolutely! Could things be worse? Sure!

No matter how great things are, they can always be better and no matter how bad things are, they could always be worse...Until you stop breathing.

Here is another thing about travel that is so eye-opening. It teaches you that you don't have to be rich, have your dream job or even much at all (Some things we consider basics) to live a fulfilling life with lots of happy times.

I've seen some of the poorest people in the world having some of the best times, making amazing memories.

There are probably plenty of things you think you need to be happy. The reality is, those are just things you want. Things that have been programmed into your mind, to make you think you need.

How much more fulfilled will having the latest iPhone make you feel vs the last year's model that you already have? Is it cool? Sure. Will it make you happy? Temporarily. Will it make you fulfilled? Absolutely not!

So, thank the universe every day that you live when you do, where you do. It makes it that much easier to live a fulfilling life. To chart the path to your own destiny. Never give away your power to anyone.

Whenever you put the blame on someone or something for whatever you feel is lacking in your life, you are also giving away your ability to change it. As long as you are living in the free world, you always have the ability to change your situation.

Jealousy and envy of other people's lives will only make you miserable.

This is one of the things I caution about with social media. It has almost turned into a competition to see who can make more people jealous of their (typically fake) lifestyle.

Why would you want to participate in that? What is inside of you that drives you to make other people, people you don't even know in many cases, jealous? Look inside yourself and I will guarantee it's because of something you were lacking as a child or that you are lacking now.

There is a void in your soul that you are looking to fill. I'm not saying this to be insulting or judgmental.

Honestly, look inside yourself. Trying to make yourself feel better by making others feel worse will never lead to fulfillment.

To live a fulfilling life, you must be thankful for the life you live, the people you're lucky enough to share it with and all the things you have.

Never take a second for granted! It can all come crashing down at any moment.

Life is full of surprises. That is why surprise is one of the 8 primary human emotions.

If the worst does happen and the world as you now know it comes to an end, appreciate that you are still breathing and do your best to rebuild.

Knowing that you have the power to shape your destiny is a gift in itself. At least be grateful for that!

RULE 18: FIND BEAUTY IN THE LITTLE THINGS!

The main takeaway from this rule is that to live a fulfilling life, you need to slow down occasionally. There is beauty all around us and when you slow down to recognize this, when you start noticing the beauty in the little things, it instantly boosts your mood.

The culture of most Americans is very fast-paced compared to the rest of the world.

My wife is originally from Europe. One day, before we eventually decided to get married on an island in Belize, we were looking for a wedding venue in Santa Cruz, CA.

It was not far from where we were living at the time and there are lots of scenic places along the coastline. We decided to bring her parents along to spend the day with us.

There is a little coffee shop in the town of Los Gatos, California that was our favorite. We would always stop there first before heading to the beach. It was a scenic twenty-minute drive, over the foothills and through a redwood forest and we would enjoy our coffee along the way.

As usual, we stopped at our favorite coffee shop, this time with her parents (We'd had many meals together but this was our first coffee stop). When we ordered our coffee to go, they were legitimately confused.

To them, ordering coffee was not something you just grabbed on the way to do something else, for a burst of caffeine. When you stop at a coffee shop, you sit down together at a table, drink your coffee slowly and talk with each other - EVERY TIME!

I'm not making an argument for or against however you'd like to drink your coffee. I enjoy drinking a cup of coffee while driving. I also like having conversations while driving. That could be more to do with the car culture of America than anything.

I'm more comfortable in my car than just about anywhere. The point is that I, as an American, am pre-programmed to be on-the-go, all the time.

I also noticed that they tended to do everything slower. Not intentionally or due to any kind of disability, they would just notice things I would speed past without regard to. They would literally, "Stop and smell the roses".

This has not changed in them, no matter how long they have lived in the USA. That part of their culture has been so ingrained, they have managed to escape the Bay Area rat race mentality, almost entirely.

Something increasingly vital to enjoying the beautiful, Mediterranean climate and landscape.

My father-in-law is also a micro-robotics engineer. This says something about his personality and may contribute towards their immunity to, "Life in the fast lane".

You can't rush things in his profession and you must work methodically and systematically. There is no room for error. It forces you to, at the very least, notice the little things, if not find beauty in them.

I have seen a similar mentality in my travels just about anywhere outside of the United States. If you can find the right balance, between slowing down, finding the beauty in the little things and being efficient and productive, that is perfection.

Slowing down to appreciate the beauty in the little things can also be taken to the extreme. While it may be good for you personally, all the time, it is not necessarily good for society, business and productivity all of the time. There must be a balance.

Believe it or not, there really is such a thing as, "Island time." "Island time" also extends to many countries in Latin America (Though not all of them).

When I lived in Ecuador, there were only about two hours in any given day, that you could really count on getting anything productive done. They were between 10 am and 11 am, then between 2 pm and 3 pm.

The rest of the time, the person you really needed to see was either coming in late, taking an early/long lunch or leaving early.

There must be a balance between personal and societal fulfillment. If you happen to know where that exists in perfect form, please let me know so I can travel there and see it in action for myself.

RULE 19: LET YOURSELF BE AMAZED/EXCITED BY THE BIG THINGS!

It's easy in life to become jaded. Especially in the modern world that we live in. We have become spoiled by technology.

All you need is your phone, a cardboard headset and you can virtually project yourself anywhere in the world, doing anything. Scratch that - Even out of this world.

Do you want to explore the moon, fly in a fighter jet, ride a donkey deep into the Grand Canyon or feel nauseous on the biggest rollercoaster ever built? You can do them all from the comfort of your own living room.

Just about anything you can think of doing, or anyplace you would like to see, you can, with virtual and augmented reality.

As amazing and real as these experiences feel now, this technology is still in its infancy. Let yourself be amazed by it. Imagine you living 100 years ago and finding this technology just laying around somewhere... You would literally flip the fuck out! This is put mildly.

No matter how authentic technology can make something feel, it will never be a true substitution for the real thing. We must understand this yet also try our hardest to not become spoiled by the great achievements of man. We must also never stop appreciating the beauty of the natural world.

Travel to the Grand Canyon, sit on a beach and lose yourself, staring into the vastness of the ocean, travel to the highest peak you can find and climb it.

When speaking of the great achievements of man, let us remember the achievements of the ancient past as well.

If you ever travel to the Yucatan peninsula, do yourself a favor and skip Chichen Itza and the ruins of Tulum. They are overly crowded and cleaned up to look almost like a Disney attraction.

If you must see one of them, the turquoise sea just below the ruins of Tulum is a special combination, granted there is no pyramid.

If a pyramid is what you want to see in Mexico, rent a car or take a tour to Coba. The first thing you will notice is that it feels very remote...

because it is. It is also not very crowded. You can rent a bike for a few dollars and take yourself on a tour of an ancient, Mayan civilization, riding along a jungle trail, stopping to explore, touch and feel many different ruins, some only partially excavated.

You can even live out your childhood Tarzan fantasies, hanging from giant vines all around you.

When you reach the end of the trail, you will see the main pyramid towering out of the jungle like a skyscraper. The best part, for now, you can climb to the top.

If this view, combined with the experience doesn't amaze you, stop taking selfie after selfie and start living by more of the 36 rules to fulfillment... Immediately. This is a moment you should savor for the rest of your life.

Another theme you might notice by now is that to have a fulfilling life, you need to gain experiences. Gain as many experiences as you can.

To let yourself be amazed/excited by the big things, you must get out and see/experience the big things.

If you want to feel truly fulfilled, you must allow yourself to truly feel your experiences. That means not having a, "Too cool for school" attitude. When you see something that makes you want to jump up and down with genuine excitement, jump up and down with excitement.

No one will look negatively upon you if you do. Excitement is contagious. If anything, you will just spread your excitement and make others feel comfortable expressing how amazed and excited they really are.

If anyone does happen to look upon you negatively, for being excited about something that anyone could/should be excited about, that is their problem. That is the negativity in their life shining through for all to see. Take pity on them.

With enough excitement, you can even make these people crack a smile of joy from time to time. I know life can be hard and will beat you down if you let it. Don't let it!

As adults, it's our duty to teach our children whatever we can. That is how knowledge has been passed down from generation to generation.

We are not the only purveyors of knowledge however... Just because we're a little taller and a little older, there are many things our children can teach us, things that we have forgotten. Let yourself be amazed/excited by the big things.

Go to the zoo or amusement park or natural wonder of your area and watch them be amazed. There is no reason you shouldn't act just as excited as them!

RULE 20: LET YOUR INNER CHILD OUT TO PLAY!

No matter how old you are or how old you feel, we all have an inner child just waiting to burst out. It's that impulsive little devil, sitting on top of your left shoulder, telling you to just throw caution to the wind and do something fun, albeit potentially inappropriate or a little dangerous.

You'll want to be a little careful with this rule, as it can run contrary to others, depending upon how and when you let this little devil make the decisions.

Obviously, do not harm others and try not to do anything to cause yourself irreparable harm. It might take a little training depending upon your willpower and experience, so start slow at first.

Maybe you're not much of a drinker but on occasion, while out with friends, you decide to indulge in a cocktail or two. You feel a little warm, a little looser than normal and laugh at jokes you might not otherwise.

You let yourself come out of your normal, day to day shell, so to speak. This may be one example for someone. Just make sure you have a safe ride home.

Others might let their inner child out to play through extreme sports like skydiving, mountain biking, rock climbing or alpine skiing. Skiing is a big one for me during the winter, as I've already mentioned.

When I'm at the top of a double black diamond, planning my route down a steep couloir or carving GS turns at 50+ MPH, all the troubles of being an adult just disappear.

Your mind is clear, exhilarated and in the moment. It must be. One wrong move, one wrong slip or caught edge and you could end up in some serious trouble...Or worse.

This clarity is what it is like being a child again, with no real worries except what is immediately in front of you. It's also a great exercise for your body, so if you don't get hurt, it's a healthy release.

I'm not advocating strapping on a pair of skis and going crazy. I've had extensive training and over 35 years of experience in the sport. The risk for me is still very real but it's a calculated risk.

This is one of the reasons people feel so refreshed, recharged and exhilarated after a vacation. When people are in a strange place, surrounded by strange people and don't feel the same responsibility of their day to day lives, it becomes almost natural to let your inner child out to play.

You get up when you want to, take a nap if you feel like it, do cannonballs into the pool and explore where you want to. These are things that children do all the time and they feel damn good, especially as an adult.

I mentioned that my wife and I got married in Belize and that our initial plan was to do a big, typical wedding near our home with tons and tons of people. Soon, what was supposed to be one of the most joyous occasions of our lives started becoming a huge ball of stress, with one headache after another.

All the date restrictions by different family members, dealing with divorced parents spouses and so on and so forth. Then came, who do we want to invite and who do we have to invite? We looked at each other and said, "Why are we doing this?"

Not, "Why are we getting married?" we already knew that answer. Why were we trying to make this about everyone else when it was supposed to be our special day?

In that moment, we decided, "Fuck it! Let's do whatever we want" also, "So we don't hurt anyone's feelings in particular, let's not invite anyone." We let the little devil win. It turned into one of the best decisions we have ever made.

We didn't just elope and we told everyone of our plans long before we left. We had an actual ceremony on the beach with a minister, music, proper wedding attire, professional photographer, a tropical bouquet and excellent champagne.

While we didn't have any, "Invited guests", we had a crowd of fellow vacationer's form that watched us recite our vows. Not because they felt obligated to be there but because they wanted to witness a special moment in the lives of perfect strangers.

No practice rehearsal, no one judging this choice or that choice, just pure positive energy. One couple was celebrating their 25th anniversary, that same day and had gotten married in the exact same spot we did.

We drove around the island on a golf cart, had a fancy dinner sitting at the best table of a gorgeous, beachfront restaurant. Random people we didn't know were sending us bottles of champagne and well wishes.

We even met the Belizean Minister of Tourism who wished us a happy union and bought us drinks.

After dinner, we drove our golf cart to a secluded part of the island, drank some more champagne and danced together under the stars. Just the two of us. It was the perfect evening and as romantic as anyone could ever hope for.

We also started out our lives together in a tropical paradise, without any stress. The only emotion we felt was love for each other. What more could you ask for?

We spent our whole trip living like children, exploring a new land, completely carefree. Not having to worry about anyone but ourselves.

One day we were driving down a jungle path and reached a fork in the road. A sign made from cardboard saying, "Beach Bar" with an arrow, written in red paint, was nailed to a post. What were we to do? You only live once!

As we made our way towards this, "Beach bar" driving further into the bush, the trail narrowed. We thought, we're either going to be murdered or this is going to be amazing.

Luckily, it was the latter. A beautiful resort-like atmosphere, friendly staff, white sand beaches as far as the eye could see, turquoise water, delicious drinks, and amazing tapas. I learned later that it had been rated one of the top beach bars in the world.

Did we make a selfish, childish decision? Some might think so. Was anyone really hurt be our decision? Not at all. Most everyone understood our motives and generally, were only happy for us. Not to mention the financial benefit.

Our wedding/honeymoon was not cheap by any means. We pampered ourselves every day with an oceanfront suite, eating at the best restaurants and drinking at the nicest bars, dancing our nights away, taking private tours, snorkeling, swimming with sharks, enjoying the spa... whatever we wanted to do. Altogether, it was still far under $10k. That's virtually unheard of for a wedding these days.

To be totally honest, we did get a few gripes from a few people. Would we still make the same decision? In a heartbeat.

Those 10 days will go down as some of the best in our lives. Another thing, many of those friends who weren't initially thrilled with our decision, finally told us in secret, that they wished they would have done the same thing we did.

So, to live a truly fulfilling life, you should give in to temptation from time to time, like a child. It might not always be the most righteous path, just know that no one is perfect.

Let your inner child out to play, or at least make a few decisions every now and then.

Don't live a selfish life. That runs counter to everything I'm trying to teach you. Just know that occasionally, it's healthy to act on your impulses. Take the road less traveled. Do what you know you want to do and jump out of that airplane already.

Please remember, don't go too crazy, don't harm anyone else, try not to harm yourself and don't make it a habit if it has the potential to become addicting/unhealthy.

RULE 21: BELIEVE IN MAGIC, IF ONLY FOR FUN!

This is not a make or break rule! If you're a scientist or completely focused on the laws of physics as we currently know them, I probably won't be able to change your mind.

Though one thing that does change, probably more often than you would like to admit, is scientific opinion or, "Fact" as we like to call it. I put, "Fact" in quotes because facts shouldn't change. They should be immutable and unquestionable, by definition.

Yet, as we learn more and more about the universe we inhabit, our ideas, our consensus of reality is ever changing. What's good for you one year will kill you the next. A few years later, we learn it's not only good again, it's practically essential, and so it goes. This happens with nearly everything.

So... To get back to rule 21...Why not? A lot of people find joy in believing real magic exists in the world. Maybe it does. We've always looked at phenomena we couldn't explain as magical...Or of the gods.

There are a lot of things we don't completely understand and call, "Pseudoscience's" like astrology, crystal healing, tarot cards, palm reading, basically all the occult. Is it a placebo or is there something behind it?

Do a quick search online or read the comments of any YouTube Astrologer. Pseudoscience or not, they bring many people joy and hope.

Hope they might not otherwise have while going through difficult times in their lives.

In this way, I look at it almost like religion. If it doesn't do you or anyone else harm, believe in whatever you want to believe in.

Eastern medicine and herbalism were once scoffed at and those treating patients with such methods were quickly dismissed, labeled as quacks. Modern, western medicine has been recently considering the validity and efficacy of some of those treatments with seriousness (By recently, I'm talking about the last 10 years or so).

Not surprising, to the long believers, many of these treatments are being backed up with double-blind studies, found therapeutic and effective.

Even if some treatments are not as effective as modern pharmaceuticals or surgical alternatives, many are now being considered effective prophylactics.

In any case, wouldn't it be cool to know there were other, parallel dimensions with completely different laws of physics? Lands filled with witches and warlocks, battling it out between good and evil. I think that's part of the draw to the paranormal.

There is still a lot we don't know about the universe. A whole lot! Who knows, maybe someday we'll learn that these crazy, paranormal pseudoscience's aren't so crazy after all.

Until then, if it doesn't directly make your life more fulfilling, it might make it a little more fun, which if had in a healthy way, indirectly leads to greater fulfillment.

RULE 22: LEARN TO LET GO OF NEGATIVE EMOTIONS FROM SITUATIONS THAT NO LONGER PHYSICALLY AFFECT YOU, OR FROM SITUATIONS YOU HAVE NO POWER TO CHANGE!

This is one of those rules that are much easier said than done. The entire field of psychology and behavioral science was created with the main intention of learning how to do this.

Countless books, dissertations, symposiums and billions of hours of therapy, all with the intention of learning the best way to do this. With all that being said, do you think I'm even take a crack at teaching you the best way to do this? Not exactly.

I am going to tell you to do your best to find the root of those negative emotions. If you are very self-aware or have experienced something particularly traumatic, that may or may not be the easiest step.

Even if you can pinpoint it, there are typically things, in addition, that are not so on the surface. These are things you might never put together. Things that are causing you to have a stronger reaction to this trauma than others.

Sometimes these things happen when we are very young children, with no conscious recollection. Other times we block them out subconsciously, as a protection mechanism.

Even still, there are times it is a combination of very small instances that happen over a very long period. One thing by itself not damaging or even memorable but collectively as a whole, contributing to a negative reaction, or way of thinking you don't even realize.

In any case, professional therapy is your best bet here. You can try and work through it all by yourself, or with friends and family. Sometimes that can be effective but most people are in therapy because that didn't help as much as they'd like.

Going to therapy is not a magic bullet. You're going to need to be open and honest with your therapist, which takes trust and time to build that trust.

Maybe you can walk in the first hour of meeting your therapist and spew out a bunch of things that are bothering you, typically those are only surface issues.

If they are your main issues, really getting into the weeds, the deeper reasons and meanings to find a solution still takes time and trust.

What most people struggle with, as an unforeseen issue, is the need to be open and honest with themselves. Really looking inward and seeing those things, picking apart the things you'd rather hide away in a lockbox of your own subconscious. Things that hurt more to admit to yourself, than to anyone else.

Then, practice the exercises your therapist gives you. You're seeing them for a reason and have committed your time and money. Go back to rule 15 and trust in their authority and knowledge. Even if the first 10 exercises don't resonate, the 11th might be the one that does the trick.

Don't expect things to instantly get better. Many people go for decades before they can learn to let go of those negative emotions. Many people never stop going, even after they are, "Feeling better" for routine maintenance.

I didn't bring this up before but maybe should have. You will be spending a lot of time with this person as you go through your life. Make sure you find someone that you are comfortable with and if it's not clicking with the first one, after solid effort, don't be afraid to find another.

As difficult and complex as this rule is, without an effort to follow it, you will never be truly fulfilled. You must learn to let go of negative emotions.

If it's a situation that you are currently in and can't be changed, the only thing you can change is your perspective. A glass half full, half empty kind of thing. It's not a problem, it's a challenge and challenges build character, impart wisdom and are easier to overcome.

I know, easier said than done but you're just going to have to trust me on this one.

Sometimes the situation itself may never get better, never fully return to how it was before. In cases like these, such as paralysis or serious injury, you don't need me to tell you how tough your road ahead will be.

Your life will likely never be the same and depending upon your purpose pre-injury/illness, that may have to change as well.

No matter how serious your injury is, if it is not immediately terminal, you still need a purpose. Your purpose may even be to defy the odds and make a full recovery, if possible.

Never believe anyone who tells you it will never be possible. Even if science hasn't caught up yet, there is always hope it will.

You can still live a fulfilling life, albeit different than you once imagined. There will be bad days, there will be worse days but there will still be good days. Use those good days to give you the strength to get through the bad ones.

For some reason, you have been placed in the situation that you are in. You can wallow in self-pity or you can, "Suck it up, buttercup!"

I'm not being insensitive here so please don't get offended because you know a person with an affliction or that person with another. This is a phrase I learned from a father to a paraplegic person, it highlights the value of overcoming adversity.

Do something positive with the hand you have been dealt. You must still live your life, so make the most of it. Have the courage and strength to be an inspiration to others. Tell your story!

If that's not your thing, you don't have to put yourself in the spotlight.

You can still try and do more good than harm in this world. Just because you have faced serious adversity, you aren't getting off the hook.

You can still follow, in most cases, the 36 rules to a fulfilling life...And they will still work for you.

RULE 23: DO NOT FORGET FOND MEMORIES FROM YOUR PAST AND REMINISCE UPON THEM OFTEN!

I don't care how terrible you think your life has been, we all have at least a few fond memories from our past. These memories are a gift that time can take away, only if we let it. That is of course under normal circumstances.

Traumatic brain injuries and degenerative illness aside, if we do not reminisce upon our fond memories often, they often slip away like a feather in the wind.

Much like a feather in the wind, they may float back around from time to time on their own. You see something that reminds you of someone or something, a smell that brings you back to your childhood.

For me and many in my generation, in the USA, it's the smell of gasoline. As funny as that may sound, it brings back those fond memories. If you were a late 70s/80s child, this will probably resonate with you as well.

On a warm summer day, refueling my car can take me back to the gas dock at Lake Don Pedro, where I had some of my best memories growing up.

The smell of dirty engine oil brings me back to my late grandfather's garage, where we rebuilt a car together.

Every time I walk onto an apparatus floor of a fire station, the smell is distinct but hard to describe: Tire rubber, grease, cleaning materials, exhaust and old smoke are probably the right combination, it instantly brings me back to those happy times as a kid, visiting my dad and his buddies, getting to slide down the fire pole or take a ride on the fire engine, while they worked their usual 24-hour shifts.

Music is probably one of the best ways to travel back in time. There is something so visceral about it that brings back not only the memories but also the feelings you had, maybe at one specific time when you were listening to a certain song.

Studies even indicate that people with Alzheimer's and other types of dementia benefit from listening to music. It is thought that the disease, as debilitating as it is, has little effect on the areas of the brain linked to musical memory.

By playing music that you know gave this person fond memories, you can help them feel comfortable and relaxed or give them a joyful energy, based on the specific music you play.

It is a tool that while may not work the same for everyone, can help some reconnect with their loved ones.

Fond memories are feelings of positivity. They have the power to make you feel good both emotionally and physically. They help you appreciate the life you have and the parts you have already lived. One of the pillars of rule number 17.

You must reminisce often but also seek to make new fond memories, just as frequently.

A life looked back upon, filled with fond memories of various kinds is not only a life fulfilled but a life worth living.

This also rings true when giving people memories of you. Make them positive. Give them something to miss when you are gone. Have them look forward to seeing you again.

RULE 24: LEARN THE ART OF FORGIVENESS!

When speaking of forgiveness, there are two parts that deserve equal attention: Forgiving others and forgiving yourself.

Learning to forgive others:
Learning to forgive others makes following many the 36 rules much easier. If someone has wronged you, whether intentionally or unintentionally, holding a grudge against them will only end up hurting you in the long run. It's kind of like the Buddhist quote on anger I included earlier "...You are the one that gets burned".

Depending upon whether you choose to move past the forgiveness and continue with the relationship of the person who slighted you depends upon several things: The slight, the intention, the strength of the relationship beforehand, potential mental illness and the reputation of the person that slighted you.

You may want to forgive them in your heart but still not continue with the relationship if the slight was especially hard, the intention was evil and your relationship was not very strong to begin with.

You may want to forgive them and understand that they did not mean to intentionally hurt you. This is probably the case with most of negative interactions and hurt feelings we have with the people we care for. In these cases, be quick to forgive and try to forget.

If this behavior is especially unhealthy and becomes a pattern, do not let them closer than arm's length. Forgive them but do not give them the opportunity to continuously harm you. That is a fool's errand.

Sometimes, you may not even know the person who attempted to do you or your loved ones wrong. They may be total strangers and criminals with the worst intent.

I have heard many stories of families forgiving the killers of their spouses, sisters, brothers or even children. In all honesty, they have much more strength than me.

While admiring their ability to forgive, that takes a certain fortitude that I freely admit to not possessing. It may be a character flaw within myself, a desire for vengeance? That would likely be the most honest answer, as much as I would like to say it was about justice and protecting others in the future.

On May 13, 1981, exactly one year before I was born, an assassination attempt was made on Pope John Paul the 2nd's life. The Man who attempted the assassination was a Turkish citizen who had just escaped a Turkish prison where he had been recently handed down a life sentence...for murder.

Upon his escape, he made his way to Vatican City where he shot The Pope, several times and injuring him quite severely. The man was then incarcerated in an Italian prison.

After healing, Pope John Paul the 2nd made a public declaration forgiving the man. He later visited him in Jail, even becoming friends with the man's family.

Pope John Paul the 2nd eventually made a case for the man to be pardoned in Italy, which was granted. The man returned to Turkey to finish his initial sentence and even converted to Christianity.

When he was released from his Turkish prison, Pope John Paul the 2nd had already passed away from age related causes. The man who had attempted to assassinate him made a special trip to The Pope's tomb, where he laid down roses in respect, admiration and appreciation for The Pope.

This is clearly a special case. The motive for the assassination attempt has been speculated to be government related but the truth is, we may never know. The Pope was credited for helping to end communist rule in Poland and eventually all of Europe.

He also strove to create one great religious alliance between Christians, Muslims and Jews with the Catholic church at the heart of it. Many may have viewed this as controversial and many have seen his efforts as a path to world peace.

After all, they are all Abrahamic religions. Even myself, who is not religious, can recognize the great things attempted by Pope John Paul the 2nd and he was elevated to the status of Saint, posthumously by Pope Francis in 2014.

We are certainly not all saints. Not by any means. That does not mean that we do not poses saintly qualities from time to time. Forgiveness is one of these qualities.

You do not even have to tell the other person you have forgiven them, although a nice gesture. Just know that once you have completely forgiven them in your heart, a weight will be lifted from your soul.

Learning to forgive yourself:

For many, learning how to forgive yourself for the wrongs you have committed can be harder than forgiving others that have slighted you.

Carrying this weight with you for whatever wrong you have done, will prevent you from living a life of fulfillment.

Just as you must learn to let go of negative experiences committed upon you in the past, you must also learn to let go of negative things you have committed upon others.

Understanding that guilt is a learned emotion, much like disgust may assist you with this. You must be taught what is right and what is wrong and societal norms along with cultural behaviors have a lot to do with this.

Just as one may enjoy the sport of hunting, another may feel horrible guilt for shooting and killing a deer or elk. Even after the logical explanation of population control of the specific animal along with apex predators like mountain lions, whose populations grow unfettered with the population rise of prey animals. You can even explain to them how the hunting license they purchased helps preserve the natural ecosystem and clean up the habitat of the areas inhabited by those animals for generations.

To make things more complex, this same person with an aversion to hunting my love fishing. Are they not responsible for the pain, suffering and potential killing of another animal?

You can argue that the same benefits I pointed out regarding deer and elk also apply to fish, along with a much more undeveloped nervous system of the fish (as far as we currently understand it).

What it boils down to is social conditioning, cultural behaviors and what we are taught, plain and simple.

With that in mind, asking for forgiveness is a pillar in most religions for a reason. Guilt can eat us alive and drive us mad.

As illustrated in Edgar Allen Poe's The Tell-Tale-Heart, where a murderer, who thought his crime was committed in a perfect, undetectable way, with his evidence buried beneath his floor boards, would "hear" the beating of the murdered man's heart slowly driving him into madness.

In most cases, murder of any kind, man or animal is not at the center of your guilt. It is an act of selfishness committed against someone you care about that drives this guilt.

Whatever you do, do not try and rationalize this behavior. That is not accepting responsibility for your actions. That is pushing your guilt to another lockbox hidden away, within your subconscious, that will eventually manifest in other unhealthy, unfulfilling behaviors. Take responsibility, forgive yourself and make a change for the better!

There are lots of things that were honest mistakes, mistakes that any of us could have made that lead to these feelings of guilt. These are the things we must recognize for what they are, learn from them and forgive ourselves.

We must also do our best to try and not repeat them. Understand that the key takeaway is that we do our best.

We are not all saints. We are all only human and must learn to forgive ourselves.

RULE 25: NEVER LET FEAR STOP YOU FROM DOING WHAT YOU WANT OR ASKING FOR WHAT YOU NEED!

I hope this goes without saying but you can't be too careful in today's world.

I am not talking about fear from REAL threats, imminent danger or things that will unquestionably harm yourself or anyone else.

I am speaking of irrational fears, phobias and more specifically, fear of failure and rejection. There is a famous quote that even if you already know, will serve you well to hear again:

"Twenty years from now, you will be more disappointed by the things you didn't do than by the ones you did. So throw off the bowlines. Sail away from the safe harbor. Catch the trade winds in your sails. Explore. Dream. Discover." -Mark Twain

I want you to look back in your own life, twenty years ago. If you are not yet twenty, or were a very young child twenty years ago, look back ten or even five. Unless one of those things you did was an unspeakable crime, that even if you weren't caught for, have locked you in a prison of your own guilt, this quote should resonate with you.

The old saying of time healing all wounds is not true in every case but it does generally take away some of the sting. Most of the time, the mistakes you made in the past have taught you valuable lessons.

They may have even hurt pretty damn bad at the time - but through pain comes growth.

Some of the things that felt miserable while you were doing them, you now look back upon with fond memories. You probably even knew they were good for you, even while making you feel miserable.

In these situations, people with a military background like to say, "Embrace the suck!"

If you've always wanted to learn how to surf but are afraid of sharks, don't let that fear stop you. You don't need to hear the statistics of how small the actual risk of being attacked is again.

I know, I know, no matter how small the risk, for whatever it is, it will always happen to someone. Kind of like winning the world's shittiest lottery.

I've said it before and I'll say it again when it's your time, it's your time. Nothing will change that. Go take a surfing lesson already.

Is it really a fear of sharks or a fear of not knowing what is underneath you? If your fear of sharks is really bad, get your SCUBA certification and go swim alongside them. It's a lot less scary than you think and a lot more interesting, awe-inspiring even. They just swim along and most of the time, pay no attention to you.

In my first real open-water dive, I had the privilege of seeing two reef sharks mating in their natural habitat. We all swam along near them like some creepy shark porn voyeurs but it was a pretty cool experience and one I haven't had since. More to the point, not the least bit frightening.

As a Paramedic, I saw a lot of things that made me question life, death, the choices we make and the choices that are made for us. I will tell you a quick story of one such case but will omit/change some of the details due to HIPPA laws and to respect the privacy of the man and his family.

I was working in the ER when a man in his early twenties was brought in by ambulance. He was unconscious from a severe head injury. This young man was also a semi-pro level athlete in a pretty extreme, often dangerous sport.

After helping to stabilize him, we wheeled him to the ICU and I learned that he had plans to go do this sport with his friends that morning. When he didn't show up to meet them and they couldn't reach him by phone, they became worried and went to check on him.

When they arrived at his house, they found him lying on the ground in his kitchen, breathing and with a pulse but unconscious and coagulated blood pooled on the ground under his head.

I can't tell you if he lived or died, unfortunately. If he did survive, he had a long road to recovery and very likely, would never be the same.

Most of the time, I didn't follow up after they left our immediate care. It felt healthier not to become too emotionally involved.

This is one of the many stories I have, of an experience that made me realize when it's your time, it's your time.

It didn't happen to him doing anything different than everyone does every day, even though he was an incredibly healthy, in-shape, extreme athlete. Even though he was even going to participate in that extreme sport the very next morning.

That next morning was not his time. For whatever reason, it was not meant to happen then, it was meant to happen the night before, in the "Safety" of his home. So please, never let fear stand in the way of doing whatever it is that you really want to do.

Even if it's just asking that girl or guy you really like on a date. The worst that could happen is they say no. If you don't ask, you will never know their answer. That is far worse.

What if they would have said yes? What if they were, "The one"? It's those, "What if's" that Mark Twain spoke of, that lead to regret and disappointment.

Remember, this is a two-part rule and the second is just as important: Never be afraid of asking for what you need.

It has been proven that part of the reason for the gender pay gap is that women are less likely to try and negotiate a job offer for a higher wage or greater benefits than men.

This is rooted in fear and self-doubt. False thinking that if you come across as, "Difficult" they will change their minds about you. This couldn't be further from the truth.

The moment you receive a new job offer, you will never have more power in that employer/employee relationship. They want you! They need you! They just told you so. They are also, most likely expecting you to negotiate. I have hired lots of people in my time. I want to see your negotiating skills.

If you won't even fight for yourself, for what you want or need, what makes me think that you will fight for the needs of my company? What makes me think that you're the right person to negotiate this contract or that contract later down the road?

Even if you're not in a position to be negotiating contracts, it is likely that at some point, you will be put in a position to decide on behalf of the company. I want to know you will do everything you can to make the best possible decision.

I once negotiated my salary up nearly double what the initial offer was. It took several days of back and forth but I got the pay I wanted. I was also able to get extra benefits thrown in that no one else in the entire company had.

I wasn't playing any games with them. That is not my negotiating style and I love to negotiate. I was straightforward and absolutely prepared to walk away if I didn't get what I did as a minimum.

There is no place for self-doubt and regrets in a fulfilled life. Never let fear stand in your way!

RULE 26: TRY YOUR BEST NOT TO JUDGE OTHERS!

This rule sounds a lot like, "Judge not, that ye be not judged." While it's true that at the core, it's a little King Jamesy, I'm not going to pull any more direct quotes from the bible or any other religious book.

Also, please remember what I said in the preface, a good piece of advice is a good piece of advice, no matter what the source.

We also live in a world filled with different cultures and customs. What some may consider a normal way of life, others might find horrifying. How can you not judge the practice of honor killings?

At some point, as the world gets smaller and smaller, we will eventually need to decide upon a list of values that we can all share. Just as all cultures are different, some do certain things better or worse than others. If we can only take the good things from every culture and drop the bad stuff, world peace might finally be attainable.

I realize this is utopic, completely unrealistic and would take a miracle of epic proportions.

Even if this utopic, dare I say enlightened world could one day exist, it will certainly not be in my lifetime or in the lifetime of many generations to come. This is the biggest problem with the concept of a borderless world.

As divided as we are in the west alone, how can we even imagine everyone in the world living together, side by side in perfect harmony?

The best we can hope for at this point is tolerance for western views of non-barbaric customs. The problem with that is, we can't even agree on what is barbaric and what is not barbaric in the west anymore.

A big one is the topic of abortion. Is it the barbaric killing of an innocent child or a woman's right to choose what happens within her own body? No matter the stage of fetal development? If you think it's barbaric, do you think it's always barbaric, in every circumstance? Even in cases of rape or incest? Where the woman's life is in danger? If you believe it to be a woman's right to choose, do you think there should be a moralistic cutoff in fetal development?

Is there some middle ground most of us can agree upon without partisan bias or religious pressure?

I think abortion should be safe, legal and rare. I also think there should be a moralistic cutoff point, before the end of the first trimester, unless exigent circumstances exist. Three months should be plenty of time to know you are pregnant and make a choice.

I also think the father should get to play some sort of a role in that choice if you were equally responsible for the irresponsible behavior that caused an unintended pregnancy.

There should be no law that forces the mother to carry the baby to term or abort it without his consent, but his opinion should be taken into serious consideration.

The mother's choice affects more than just her. He will also have to live his entire life with, "What ifs" if she chooses to abort her pregnancy without having the courtesy to ask how he feels.

This is just my opinion and an idea of what compromise might look like. There should be no outright winners in compromise.

Each party should feel equally happy and equally unhappy. If you know this going in, it is a lot easier.

If you are completely against abortion, are you also against the morning after pill (Essentially a high dosage of regular birth control hormones to prevent fertilization and development of a zygote from ever taking place)? Are you also against regular forms of birth control?

If so, you are letting your personal or religious views interfere with the lives of others, through your support in developing public policy.

Neither of the above cases has anything to do with abortion or the killing of a fetus. In fact, they prevent the need for abortion when used correctly.

I can at least understand your argument against abortion. The morals surrounding when life begins are subjective. This now, however, just became a debate about outdated, puritanical ideals.

Would it not scare you if you were being bound by the strict, outdated, fundamentalist laws of another belief system that you did not agree with?

If we ever want to have a chance at coming back together as a society, this rule, along with the rest laid out in this book, are of great importance.

Getting back to a less philosophical view, speaking only to western culture, there are two reasons for trying your best not to judge others and are somewhat interconnected.

The first reason is that we have all made mistakes at some point or another. We were all raised with different values, under different circumstances and at different times.

While true that we should learn from mistakes of the past, trying to empathize with the actions of another is much healthier than judgment.

Try to understand why they made the decision they did. Do this before immediately judging them for making a choice you don't think you would have made.

Once you start getting into the habit, the pattern of judging others is hard to break. You start seeing bad decisions everywhere. I guarantee if you continue down this road, you will eventually judge someone for something that you have done yourself.

You will probably do this many times, justifying your reasoning for making that same decision while chastising them for theirs simultaneously. This leads to a very negative attitude and frame of mind.

Some people judge others to make themselves feel better about themselves. This brings me to the second reason you can't live a fulfilling life while being judgmental.

There is something that happens to your own self-confidence when you start picking apart other people.

In what was first an attempt to make you feel better about yourself, you start believing everyone is judging you, just as you are to them.

While this may or may not be true, having this awareness, even false awareness, leads you to start judging yourself. Judging yourself in the same negative way that you have been judging everyone else.

Those who are living a fulfilling life do not concern themselves with the actions of others, if their actions do not directly and negatively affect them or those they love.

When the actions of others do negatively affect them, they deal with it as healthy and immediately as possible. They are self-aware but also self-confident. Their self-awareness comes from their self-confidence.

Their self-confidence comes from the ability to objectively view themselves and others with compassion.

If you harbor negative emotions towards others, those negative emotions will come straight back to you. It's the old, "I am rubber, you are glue, it bounces off me and sticks to you" saying from our childhood.

Maybe you thought of it as just a stupid comeback to an insult but it rings true, even as adults.

We are all only one bad decision, one twist of fate or a seemingly innocent mistake, from ending up in jail. Branded criminals! Most people commit crimes daily without even realizing it.

Therefore, should we still judge everyone with a criminal record, even first time, low-level offenders as bad people? I will leave you to ponder this question using your own best judgment.

RULE 27: TRY AND DO MORE GOOD THAN HARM!

There is a saying used by campers and other people who love the outdoors, "If you pack it in, pack it out and leave your campground/trail in better shape than you found it".

This is a great metaphor for life in general. We should not only hear it more often, but we should also do more to live by those words every day.

Doing good is the one shortcut to happiness that always leads to fulfillment if done with the right intentions. Although still good for society, please don't do good things just to brag about what a good person you are. This is the only way doing good deeds will not lead you to a fulfilling life.

Go out of your way to do something good, tangible, in real life, often (not just cyber, moral and emotional support). Do this without expecting anything in return and without talking about it. Certainly, without bragging about it (even the humble brag).

It will warm your soul and make someone else's life a little easier, a little better and a little brighter. Sometimes, those little things to you, that take very little effort or sacrifice, can mean the world to someone else.

There are many stories of people offering seemingly small acts of kindness, that have made a grand impact in the lives of others.

Offering moral and emotional support to others is not bad. There are many times in people's lives when they legitimately need that support.

When that time comes, listen to them, validate their feelings and show empathy for what they are going through. When done correctly, you are leaving that person in better shape than you found them, if only a little bit.

Can you see the difference in that and posting, "I'm thinking about you" or, "I'll keep you in my prayers" on someone's social media page?

That often comes off as patronizing and insincere, though maybe given with the best of intentions. It's just so easy to do and many people do it thoughtlessly.

As far as we know, we only have one life to live. Do you know the meaning of this life? A lot of people will claim, using a very official sounding voice, "To procreate of course."

While that is absolute for keeping our species alive, it still does not explain why we are here. That is a question we may never know the answer to.

However, after many years of studying people and humanity, I can honestly say, with complete certainty, I have learned the rules to fulfillment.

You may read this book and look critically at me, my writing style or my views on life. You may even call me a hypocrite, as I have deviated from my own rules many times throughout my life. None of this bothers me at all.

I have written this book to help people and do more good than harm. I have also stated that while you should do your best to live by these rules, that they will bring you fulfillment, we are all imperfect.

No matter how hard we try, it is impossible for most of us to live by all 36 rules, all the time. Even, dare I say... Especially for myself.

We don't always do what we know is best for us. Sometimes we do things we know for a fact are flat out unhealthy.

If I can only get you to follow one rule from this entire book, please let it be this one. Please live your entire life by this one. Do more good than harm!

Leave the path you make, the trail you blaze through life, in better shape than you found it.

RULE 28: CARE LESS ABOUT WHAT OTHER PEOPLE THINK OF YOU!

This is one rule that I'm sure we all wish we would have known when we were younger.

Many of us made stupid mistakes or wasted too much time trying to do something or be someone we were not. Trying to impress the wrong people. People you look back on and don't really care about as an adult.

Even college kids, ehem, I mean "Adults" are susceptible to this. Have you ever been to a protest or rally just because your friends were going? Even though you may not be completely educated on the topic of why you should or shouldn't be upset or enthusiastic? One that if you had more information on, you might support instead of protest? Or protest instead of support?

Luckily, most of us will grow out of this thought process. The older we get, the less fucks we tend to give.

This rule is more about caring less about what the wrong or inconsequential people think of you. There will be plenty of people throughout your life that you legitimately care about and in turn, should care about what these people think of you.

For instance, you shouldn't show up to an important job interview dressed like a slob. That violates rule 15, by not showing proper respect to their authority, position, and experience.

Maybe you made the decision to dedicate your life to a certain career, that you hate, just to make your parents proud of you. Do you question your religion but still go through the motions because you are afraid of what your family or community might say? Are you gay but afraid to come out?

These are all major blockages on your path to a fulfilling life. While we should care about what our parents, true friends or religious leaders think of us, there are certain times we must have the courage to be honest with them about who we really are.

Even if they might not be thrilled or there are consequences stemming from what you tell them.

To live a fulfilling life, you must be free to follow your own path to fulfillment. The 36 rules are relevant to everyone because they merely guide you to be your best self, whatever that may be.

Also realize that you have many versions of yourself, depending upon the situation. I'm not talking about being fake, I'm talking about being appropriate. (Think about the job interview I already mentioned. You are still you, just a more polished version that is more appropriate to the situation.)

If you happen to be a teenager or younger while reading this book, I apologize for some of the colorful language I use. You shouldn't talk like that... at least not around the grown-ups.

You have your whole life ahead of you, pursue your passions, learn as much as you can and try to care less about what other people think of you.

If you're already an adult, you should just invent a time-machine and go back to visit your younger self. Tell yourself to stop caring what inconsequential people think of you. Tell yourself in ten years or less, you will be an entirely different person and what will make you cool then is way different than what makes you cool now.

One more thing, bring yourself a sports almanac like in "Back to The Future 2". That way you can grow up and turn into a rich asshole like Biff. On second thought, don't turn into a rich asshole like Biff. That kind of defeats the whole purpose of this book.

For the few of you who need a little extra "help" to be your best self. Those that are reading this book for the wrong reasons, you may want to start thinking about other people a little more and yourself a little less. Also, please don't invent a time-machine.

RULE 29: LET YOURSELF FEEL YOUR EMOTIONS BUT REALIZE THAT THEY MAY NOT ALWAYS BE AN ACCURATE DEPICTION OF REALITY!

In past generations, there have been, stereotypically two types of people. The stoic, logical man and the emotional, irrational woman.

The logical thinker has a top-down approach to their emotions. They first understood exactly what happened in their brain and the brain would tell their heart how it should feel. That process usually made it harder for them to outwardly show how they felt.

The emotional thinker has a bottom-up approach. They first felt their emotions with their heart, reacted to the emotion outwardly and then processed it logically with their brains. (I hope you understand this is clearly biological metaphor)

"Top downers" tend to bottle up their emotions more, causing actual physical harm to themselves.

By not releasing their emotions in a healthy way, they tend to have higher cortisol levels which increase weight, belly fat, raises blood pressure and a whole host of other health problems. However, they tend to make better, more well thought out decisions that are less impulsive.

The, "Bottom uppers" release every emotion they have inside. Sometimes letting hurtful words fly out of their mouths before their brains can process what they're really saying.

This is good for their own personal health but bad for the people taking the brunt of it. "Bottom uppers" also tend to make decisions based upon how they feel more than how they think. This makes them easier to manipulate and emotional decisions can be impulsive decisions.

On the plus side, "Bottom uppers" also tend to be more comfortable outwardly showing compassion and empathy than, "Top downers".

In the modern world, we are in the process of an emotional/logical evolution. They are not necessarily based upon gender stereotypes anymore. Men are more comfortable showing their feelings and talking about their emotions. Women are feeling more comfortable showing off their intelligence and professional skills.

Because we are in the PROCESS of this evolution, one that goes against biological and social conditioning, since the beginning of humankind, we are bound to make a few mistakes from time to time.

We may not realize that our emotions are not always an accurate depiction of reality. Sometimes men can come across as overly emotional, more that the situation calls for.

Sometimes, it might serve women to be a little less tactful and little more emotional, in the way they deliver certain information in the workplace. When I say a little more emotional, I mean a little more genuine.

If you are a woman and don't fit the emotional stereotype, don't try and fake emotions. That comes across just as disingenuous. I will show you two examples of this playing out on opposite ends of the spectrum.

We all know or have seen enough man-bun wearing, overly emotional, "Soy boys" so I think you have a clear perception of this example/stereotype.

I understand why there is a tendency for women to want to overcompensate their masculinity, to feel heard and respected as equals amongst their male counterparts. The truth is, you are already respected by most of men as equals.

We live in a world where multiple generations are accustomed to - No! Expecting to see women in the office, in positions of power. This is normal to everyone now. When you overcompensate, it comes off as disingenuous.

Disingenuous people are unlikable people no matter what their sex. Think of Elizabeth Holmes, the disgraced former CEO of the defunct, scam company, Theranos.

She even tried to deepen her voice in the workplace to sound more masculine. She was unlikable, not that she cared. Her idol was Steve Jobs for crying out loud.

We've all heard people say the derogatory term, "Short man's syndrome" to describe a very similar, disingenuous overcompensation in certain, height challenged men.

This has been discussed by many who have said coming across as, "Disingenuous and unlikeable," were Hillary Clinton's two biggest problems in the 2016 election. When she came across as a no-nonsense, powerful woman, that felt genuine to me. I could trust that. It didn't make her unlikable in my eyes at all.

She has never been as naturally likable as her charismatic husband, Bill. Not many people are.

When she tried to seem "likable", showing clearly forced smiles, it felt fake to me. She looked more like Cruella de Vil, trying to hide the fact that she was planning on skinning a bunch of puppies for their fur, as soon as she was out of the spotlight. That is what made her feel disingenuous, unlikable and untrustworthy to many.

Trump came across like a blowhard, a womanizer but at least he came across as a genuine blowhard, womanizer. I know it's 2019 but look back through our political history... even to this day. Politics has always been filled with blowhard, womanizers. On both sides of the aisle. All over the world and that is reality.

I'm not saying it's right. I'm just calling a spade a spade. Many have just been better at hiding it than Trump. I think that's partially why he was easier to accept for the majority of states in this country.

The more garbage that was dug up on his womanizing ways, just confirmed what he never really denied. That he was a womanizer and basically took pride in it.

We can all pretend to be shocked and appalled or we can all just be honest. We should say that while not a great example, his behavior wasn't unexpected.

Most men have always wanted power to get beautiful women and most women have always wanted men with power. It's in our DNA to pass on strong genetics. It also aided in survival for most of humankind.

This is changing, especially if the number of women in positions of power surpasses men. The "Trophy husband" might become more common. That would be more or a simple role reversal that detriment to society.

The worst outcome will be if more women will remain single, looking for a man with more power than she, in a dwindling pool, out of genetic predisposition and centuries of human conditioning.

The biological call to procreate and nurture are powerful forces, so we will see how this plays out. If you do decide to have a child, please be in a committed/married relationship.

We want more fulfilled people not less. We know the outcome for children in two-parent households is much better than in single parent households.

I'm doing my best to keep this as apolitical as I can. That is what I promised you in the preface, to do my best. So many of our current issues are tangled in with politics, it makes it difficult to avoid them completely.

I'm also about as middle of the road, vote on the issue, moderate as you can get. So please keep that in mind before you start to have preconceived notions about my political intentions.

I don't have a serious pony in the race and probably never will, unless we can legitimately break from our current two-party system.

Most people now identify as independent, so it's possible that one day we may be able to choose a middle-of-the-road, 3rd party.

In any case, this evolution, like any other evolution will take time. The trick is finding the proper balance of IQ (Intelligence Quotient) with EQ (Emotional Quotient). This can be done by giving equal time and consideration for the heart and head to process emotions before reacting outwardly. Analyze the situation and then respond in an appropriate, honest, self-aware and genuine way.

The main takeaway from the above diatribe is this: Depending upon the situation, people's emotions have not always been an accurate depiction of reality. Especially how they are displayed.

As this emotional evolution continues, we can expect this to worsen before it gets better. Keep this in mind before you get offended or in a heated conflict.

It can be especially tricky to control your emotions, during a heated conflict that some might call arguing. I used to react to an insult immediately with another insult, of equal or greater proportion, without even thinking about it.

It took me a few years of practice after this realization but have developed the patience to respond in a controlled, appropriate way, rather than fan the flames.

It is always much better to defuse the situation by taking a few breaths and responding in a logical, constructive way.

Learning to have control over how you respond to certain emotions is not as hard as many of the other 36 rules. All it takes is a little self-realization and a lot of practice.

You can see the growth of this skill in children, especially from 2 to 5-year-olds so there is proof it can be done. Just continue to refine it into and throughout adulthood.

I would like to mention one other thing while on this topic. The way you feel is the way you feel. They are your emotions and no one can tell you that feeling a certain way is wrong or right. They can however give you a different perspective into the situation. Sometimes this helps you realize that what you are feeling is not always an accurate depiction of reality.

Maybe your spouse is running late from work. For some reason (I'm not going to dive into your relationship) you think they are late because they are cheating on you. When they get home, you are already pissed.

In your mind, you have imagined a whole scene of what you thought was taking place. You immediately start yelling at them. Then you see they are holding a box from your favorite bakery, which is 30 minutes out of their way. They were late because they wanted to surprise you with something special and here you are chastising them.

You immediately stop yelling because you can now see why they were late. This is an example of more information helping you see reality from a different, more accurate perspective.

RULE 30: DEVELOP A REPUTATION AS SOMEONE OF CHARACTER!

First, what is character? There are several traits that I feel make you a person of character, however, there are three I would like to focus on:

Honesty: You must earn a reputation as an honest person. Trust, as we talked about, can be a hard thing to earn.

Once you hold someone's trust, you hold with it great responsibility. Do not break their trust and do not earn a reputation as a liar. Once branded a liar, you face an uphill battle in all that you do.

Even when you are telling the truth, if you have a reputation as a liar, you will always have to work ten times harder to convince anyone of anything. I'm not going to go any further into this one any more than I already have. Just tell the truth.

Accountability: This can go hand in hand with honesty. Have accountability for the things you do. The good and the bad. You can take accountability for the good things, however do not brag about them. Do this in a matter of fact kind of way, only when asked or you otherwise find appropriate.

What is more difficult, the thing that builds character is taking accountability for your mistakes or the bad things that you have done.

Everyone makes mistakes from time to time, this is a known fact. Not everyone owns up to their mistakes. It's becoming increasingly rare to see someone do this. Take advantage of this opportunity and use your mistakes to your advantage. It takes courage to own up to your mistakes, especially if you stand to lose something from them.

One day I was working in the ER when a man was brought in via ambulance in full, cardiac arrest. There was a firefighter straddling him while riding on the gurney performing chest compressions.

During a situation like this, which we call a "Full code" or, "Code blue" in the industry, there are lots and lots of people getting involved. Probably between 10 and 20 all crammed together, trying to do this or that but all working cohesively, like a bee hive.

I was in charge of setting up a machine called a 12 lead ECG monitor. Basically, it is a machine with lots of wires, that go on very specific areas to take an accurate picture of the heart's electrical activity, from many different angles.

I hooked the patient up to the 12 lead ECG but in all the commotion, forgot to clear the last patient's name and medical record from the machine and enter John Doe because I didn't have his name yet.

The doctors really needed an ECG stat and I rushed it. I got an accurate ECG. We even ended up saving that man's life after about 10 minutes of touch and go.

However, once all the commotion had ended, I realized I had the wrong patient's information entered into the machine. To make matters worse, this information was automatically uploaded via WIFI to the previous patient's medical record.

Now here is the thing, the person who used the ECG machine before me didn't log themselves out of it. That is why the last patient's information wasn't automatically cleared.

I wasn't paying attention to the fact that I didn't have to log in, I was just trying to get the ECG. I could have said nothing. My number was not recorded and by the time anyone figured out what had happened, it would be too late for it to ever come back on me.

I knew it would be wrong for me to not take accountability. I wanted to make sure that the correct ECG went to the correct medical record. I also didn't want to get the last person in trouble, even though they didn't complete their job before me.

I went to my manager and explained to him what happened. We then went through the process to fix it and have the records moved from one place to another by a different department. It was a long process. I knew I could get in trouble but I needed to take accountability for my actions. I needed to make things right.

Luckily, I had never made a mistake before and had a good reputation during the two years I had already been working there. My Manager thanked me for coming forward and I was given a verbal warning.

I did notice when annual review time came around, my mistake was nowhere to be found on it. I was however recognized for having good character and given very high marks in every area.

Self-Sacrifice: This is a theme I have running through this entire book. It is how we fight the cancer of the, "Me! Culture."

I think many of us would put our own lives on the line to save others. Even if you don't know it or have never been in that situation. People that work in public safety or the military sign up knowing the risks are real.

My Dad did, I did, all my "brothers and sisters" in public safety and the military have and we are prepared to put our lives on the line every day. For perfect strangers.

There are also those amongst us that have never been trained, have regular lives but stop to render aid after a car crash, jump into a river to catch a child from drowning, climb down a rocky cliffside carrying their severely injured friend. These people are heroes that have put their safety on the line to help save someone else.

There are also people amongst us that you might never think of as the, "Hero type" until it's too late. These are the people, the brave students and teachers that rush an active shooter in a school, unarmed, knowing they are in the direct line of fire to save countless lives.

To those who have lost their lives to protect or save others, that is the ultimate self-sacrifice. That is humanity at its finest. You have my full admiration.

While we tend to think of those big things when we hear the term, self-sacrifice, it doesn't have to be anywhere near that level to make a difference. Simply think of others before immediately thinking of yourself.

Letting someone else have the last slice of pizza, the last beer, merge ahead of you in traffic, have the spot ahead of you in line, those are the simple things I am talking about that we should all be doing. Showing a little bit of self-sacrifice goes a long way in being seen as a person of character. At the very least, someone that is likable.

Popularity should never be your reason to be a person of character, it should only be a side effect of it. If you don't understand what I mean by this already, you will once your life starts to become more fulfilling.

RULE 31: DO NOT SPEAK CRITICALLY OF OTHERS BEHIND THEIR BACKS!

When speaking of this rule, I do not mean an assessment panel speaking about job applicants after an interview or any other legitimate reason others must be critiqued in relative privacy or when not present.

I'm talking about gossip (which we have already discussed) and speaking negatively "shit talking" (which goes against Rule 5: Be kind to others).

I hear it all the time and it always makes me feel uncomfortable. Especially when this is being done in a professional environment. Even if I happen to agree with a particular statement, let's say regarding a person's untrustworthiness, it still makes me uncomfortable.

If you have a problem with someone, have the character to approach them directly about it. We have already talked about how to be respectful during conflict, so this should not be an issue.

You will always gain more points for being straightforward than a backstabber. Points from witnesses (if there are any), people that hear about it indirectly and from the other person themselves.

Most of the time, when people do this, it happens out of frustration. It may even be an automatic reaction to an email shared with an officemate. Please resist the temptation to do this. How would you like it if people were doing this to you?

While not participating is no guarantee that other people won't speak negatively behind your back, speaking negatively behind other's backs will guarantee them not thinking twice about doing it to you.

Many times, if someone is doing something wrong, embarrassing or acting out of sorts, they could use a little direct, face to face or even over the phone talk. This is even one instance where text or messaging applications can be appropriate if you aren't comfortable approaching them directly.

Shooting over a simple, "Is everything alright, you seem a little..." will go a long way towards gaining that person's respect, their trust and by letting them know that you care. They will also be more likely to have positive interactions with you in the future.

Talking shit will always bring the opposite, especially if the person in question finds out you were a participant or worse, the instigator.

It's always better to have more allies than enemies and by being direct, not talking negatively behind others backs or even joining in when others are, you will always have more allies.

Even if you feel that by joining in, you will be bonding with the shit talkers, they will still respect you more if you stay out of it and remain a neutral party.

You don't always have to stay neutral either. If you have some information about the other person, the one people are shit talking about, that you know they wouldn't mind being shared, give the group some perspective.

By providing information regarding the behavior in question, you can defend the other person before rumors get out of control.

You should always defend those that cannot defend themselves when that defense is warranted. Even and especially if you don't have a great relationship with that person.

Your defense will get back to them many times. When it does, it will often give them a new-found respect for you, potentially turning an enemy into an ally.

RULE 32: SPEAK HIGHLY OF OTHERS, ESPECIALLY WHEN THEY ARE NOT PRESENT!

Do you know what people never get tired of hearing? Good things about themselves... If they are genuine of course.

If you become known as an optimist, unafraid of giving praise when deserved and speaking well of others, you will gain many friends and allies. This of course means more meaningful connections, likely more experiences and a much more fulfilling life.

Do you want to gain double the points for this same behavior? Speak highly of others when they aren't around to hear you.

I'm not saying that you should be doing this for points in an invisible game, you shouldn't. It should be about becoming the best person you can be. Following this rule is a great way to do it.

When you speak highly of others when they are not around, it means more than if you were saying it directly to them. When you are complimenting someone directly to their face, there is always the possibility that you are being disingenuous and have an ulterior motive.

The same can be true when they are not around but the likelihood is much lower.

Many times, just as the negative things said behind someone's back find their way to them, the positives do as well. Usually twice as fast and twice as often.

When those positive things do get back, you have likely strengthened that relationship in ways otherwise not possible. Or at least in ways much faster and with much less effort.

The people you are talking too will respect you more as well. Now knowing that you are a person that freely gives credit where credit is due.

They are also more likely to trust and confide in you. Fore they may be the one on the receiving end of your praise, at some other point in another conversation.

This rule works the same in any situation, whether professional or personal. The other person may even be at the same gathering, perhaps just not in the immediate conversation.

If you can gain a reputation as the person heaping compliments over the person flinging piles of excrement, you will have much better relationships while broadening your social and professional network.

You will also become more likely to be recommended or introduced to someone who can help you with your goals or purpose. People like to talk to people that are friendly and people like to help people that they like.

Notwithstanding a grand lotto win or run on the casino, luck is created. Luck is not happenstance as many are taught to believe. It is a combination of preparedness and opportunity.

The more people you talk to and have pleasant conversations with, the more opportunities will present themselves. The bigger your network, the more opportunities you have to talk with people.

When you speak highly of others, especially when they are not present, the bigger your network will get.

You will also have to put in the work to maintain those connections. That is something else entirely. However, by following this rule, you will be much more likely to find success and fulfillment.

RULE 33: LEARN TO DELAY GRATIFICATION!

The ability to delay gratification is the single biggest predictor of success in life.

Learning how, when and in what situations to decide if a bird in the hand is better than two in the bush is a skill.

Exactly what is your probability of being able to get the two birds out of the bush? Do you have to let the one in your hand go first? Or, is there a possibility of gaining all three? Is there is a higher possibility of losing all three if you decide to try and keep one in the hand?

A skilled poker player will sit for long periods of time, giving up minimum bet after minimum bet until he thinks he has the odds in his favor. Then he might go, "All in" to either bluff, since he has developed a pattern of folding other players have picked up on, or maybe he really does have the granddaddy, royal flush!

Those are very short-term examples and more about odds than delayed gratification but they do relate.

Delayed gratification is about having the self-control to give something up now, to have something much better later. It is true that while later is never guaranteed, you might get hit by a bus tomorrow, it is the best strategy for building a life of fulfillment.

Just like nothing worth anything is rarely easy, anything worth something is rarely immediate. Hence why get rich quick schemes rarely work.

Delayed gratification was also at the center of the famous 1970 Stanford marshmallow test.

600 children were led into a room one at a time. There was a table in the room with a snack of that child's choice sitting on it (either a marshmallow, Oreo or pretzel)

They were told that they would be left alone in the room for 15 minutes and if they didn't eat the snack before the tester returned, they would give them another treat.

A small amount ate the treat immediately after the tester left the room. Of those that tried to delay gratification, about ⅓ were successful. Age was the biggest determining factor in the success of delaying gratification in this study.

Another similar study, not done by Stanford but with children of closer age, showed the lack or presence of a father at home to be the biggest determining factor. Showing that children without a father figure were more unable to delay gratification, by far.

Combining these two studies tells us two things about how to address poverty and crime rates:

1. The ability to delay gratification is linked to maturity, which is typically developed with age. Also, those who showed the ability to delay gratification as children, had better grades in school and showed higher levels of success when tracked later in life.

2. The breakdown of the family unit (homes without a masculine figure) causes a delay or pause in maturity which makes delaying gratification more difficult.

We have already discussed how the lack of a masculine figure growing up leads to higher rates of gang participation and criminal incarceration. Many of these crimes being impulsive and attempting to obtain immediate gratification.

If we can fix the breakdown of the family unit, especially in at-risk areas, we can finally have a permanent solution to lower crime rates and decrease the poverty cycle.

As stated, the ability to delay gratification in children has been proven to be one of the greatest predictors of success later in life - established in the 1970 Stanford study.

I won't go any deeper because this is not the right forum and would be getting too far off track. However, this is a discussion that we should all feel comfortable addressing, in the right atmosphere, in an open, honest and respectful way.

On an individual level, the 36 rules to a fulfilling life will not always be easy, some will be downright hard and it may take some time to really feel the difference.

A lot of these rules have some element of self-sacrifice and delayed gratification. That's why I asked you to mark down a date, one year from now in your calendar, when we were talking about surprise being one of the eight primary emotions.

While you may start to see results almost immediately, one year should be enough time to be transformative. Also remember, when you achieve the transformation you desire, you must keep up with the behaviors that got you there.

This is a lifelong commitment, but one that you will want to make. When you start to feel true fulfillment, it will be hard to imagine yourself living any other way again.

RULE 34: SHOW GRATITUDE TO OTHERS!

This rule is kind of like rule 17, in being thankful for the life you live, the people that are in it and the things you have. While rule 17 is more about feeling this internally, rule 34 is about showing it externally.

It lets other people feel appreciated. That you recognize the kind thing they have done or the sacrifice they made for you. This rule is also tied to rule 5 regarding being kind to others.

When someone is kind to you, you should respond in a kind way. Let them know you appreciate their kindness and they are more likely to continue to pay it forward. Kindness is infectious in that way.

When someone lets you merge ahead of them in traffic, don't forget the wave in the mirror or out of the door. Even if they can't see you, make the effort.

I remember driving a huge moving truck halfway across the country, also towing a car behind it. I was driving a safe, legal speed but also driving with a purpose. I was trying to beat an incoming blizzard.

I had purchased chains for the moving truck just in case but I really didn't want to have to put them on in the cold wind and drive with them on.

When I would pass professional, "Big rig" drivers, many would give me a quick flash of their headlights to let me know once I have cleared them safely enough to merge in front of them, back to the right lane.

It was too cold for a hand out of the window wave and dark during part of the drive. There was no center mirror to wave in and even if there was, they would never be able to see it. So, I did a quick, one button push of my hazard lights, just to show my gratitude.

This is yet another childhood lesson that we all need to be reminded of from time to time. Maybe we're busy, maybe we're entitled, maybe we're jaded... There is no excuse. When someone does something nice for you, no matter how small, say, "Thank you"!

I hate that I even have to include this as a rule but is just another symptom of the, "Me! Culture" cancer. In some parts of the country, you are probably reading this with curious wonder.

For those unaware, there are still actually places in these United States where saying, "Please", "Thank you" and being chivalrous are still an everyday part of life. I commend you for keeping these basic values alive.

There have been studies that show the two most important words in the success of any long-term relationship are: Thank You! Can you believe, "Thank you" outweighs, "I love you"?

I'm not saying your continued declaration of love is not important. It is. If you do not feel like a person appreciates you, how can you feel that they love you? Love is a much stronger emotion so, "Thank you" should always come before it, at some point during the day. That is, if you want that, "I love you" to feel genuine later.

They also say, "True love is never having to say, I'm sorry." I honestly question the validity of that adage and think, "I'm sorry" should be kept ready to retrieve, as soon as you take your foot out of your mouth. See rule 6, if you forgot why that is important.

Show gratitude to others. It's not just a rule to fulfillment. The most important phrase you can say to your significant other is, "Thank you".

With that being said, let me move on to Rule 35: Be sure to marry the right person for you!

RULE 35: BE SURE TO MARRY THE RIGHT PERSON FOR YOU!

Study after study have shown the number one predictor of overall life satisfaction (Fulfillment) is based upon who you marry. Make sure you marry the right person for you.

Therefore, I don't recommend anyone get married until at least their late twenties if not early thirties. Until this time, most people don't know the right person for themselves because they don't even really know themselves yet.

At least not the person their prime child rearing, money making, matrimony building, future planning selves will become. There is a lot of maturation that happens between the ages of 21 and 31... A LOT!

Use this time to find out what you like, to learn and to build your career. Go on trips with friends, explore the world as much as you can. Open your eyes to every new experience you can take in.

You're in your twenties, you may not have a ton of money yet but you can rough it with a backpack and make it happen. You will never have this much time again, until you retire.

Once your career is in full swing and you have a family to take care of, it's way easier to find the money to travel, than the time.

Date people. Find out if you're the alpha or beta in a relationship. You will quickly learn that two alphas may create passion and fire but will burn out faster than your 22nd birthday candles.

Two betas will last a little longer than two alphas but will eventually get bored with each other. "What do you wanna do?", "I dunno know, what do you wanna do?" See what I mean?

You need to find the Yin to your Yang. There is a reason why they call the second person in a relationship, "Your other half".

Learn exactly who you are. Be happy just being yourself, by yourself. When you do know exactly what you are looking for, don't be in a hurry to find it.

You have all been on a date with someone you can tell is desperate to be in a relationship. Don't be that person. Don't just settle.

When you're desperate for anything, people tend to settle for whatever is convenient. A bird in the hand remember? It's too bad that bird has only one wing, a jagged beak and won't stop squawking.

All you need to do is to be open to finding, "The one". You also need to have realistic expectations. That does not mean settle, that means realizing you're not perfect and whoever you were meant to be with won't be perfect either.

If you feel like you're on a never-ending circle of bad date after bad date, you may not know yourself as well as you think you do. Or, you may need to be a little more realistic.

Make a list about the things you can't put up with, total deal breakers. It sounds counterintuitive, but makes finding, "The one" easier than just listing all the things you want them to have.

Remember, no one is perfect so if their imperfections aren't on your deal breaker list, maybe they don't have to have ALL the things on your, "Wants" list to still be, "The one."

Maybe you just need to give it time and stop, "Looking" all together. Everything is always harder to find when you're looking for it. You also usually find it where you least expect, when you least expect to.

Alright - Now that you've found, "The one" and you just got married, what next? Do you want to have children? If so how many?

Be aware that having children will probably make your relationship more challenging. Strike that! It will absolutely, without question, make your relationship more challenging.

Study after study always show couples happiness levels and marital satisfaction decreases after their first child. It goes down a little more after the second as well, just not as much as the first.

Those happiness levels also stay lower for a long time. We don't have children to make us happy, though do we? Kids are A TON OF WORK and can be frustrating as all hell.

They also bring you many moments of joy. Joy in places you never expected. You will also never know the definition of unconditional love until you have one. You think you do with your labradoodle or whatever pet you have but you really don't.

Do not have children thinking it will make you happy. It will probably make you miserable most of the time, especially when they are small. Have children to make your life more fulfilling.

That is what they do. Those snotty, whiny, selfish, dirty diaper making, car destroying, little monsters will not make you happy all the time but they will absolutely make your life more fulfilling. Especially as you both get older, so I'm told.

We've established that kids can stress out your marriage and if you are not married to the right person, you probably won't last more than two years after having one.

There are so many other stressors that we face day to day, coming home to your spouse and new baby in a great mood every day is impossible. It's important that the person you're with understands this, is empathetic to you or at least doesn't intentionally make your day worse. Try and do the same for them.

If you don't feel loved and appreciated in your relationship, at any given time, it's likely the other person feels the same way. Try and communicate that to each other in a healthy way. You can't control what they say but you can control how you react and what you say in return.

Marriage is a marathon, not a sprint. You will go through great stretches, tiring stretches, frustrating stretches, downright exhausting stretches, exciting stretches and hopefully, find more good in it than bad. If you can find more good in your relationship than bad, it's probably worth working for. It doesn't have to be easy, remember, nothing worth anything ever is.

There are problems in every relationship. If yours aren't major ones, do everything you can to save it. Especially if children are involved.

Hopefully, you followed the steps I have laid out above before you got married. At least some variation of them.

Remember that at one point in your relationship, you both knew, with all your hearts, that you wanted to spend the rest of your lives together.

Does the rest of your life now sound a little... extra-long? You can always find a new relationship but do you know what else you will find? New problems. Guaranteed!

Marriage is a lot like fulfillment. Neither one of them will guarantee you happiness all the time and should both be looked at like a foundation. Build it strong and keep adding to it, maintaining it as you go through life together.

You shouldn't have to worry about your foundation every day but you also shouldn't go too long between walk arounds.

If you neglect your marriage for too long, the foundation will start to show cracks. Once you get too many cracks, all it will take is one major life event to cause it to crash down.

Before that, only you can say when there are too many cracks to where it's not worth repairing. Do not make that decision hastily. Do not make it due to outside influences.

Understand what a major life decision you are making and that it will affect many people.

Know that when you rip apart the foundation of your marriage, it also rips off a large part of your own foundation of fulfillment. They have become somewhat bound together by now. That takes time to repair.

Only you can say if it will be worth it in the end.

RULE 36: EVERYTHING IS ABOUT PERSPECTIVE!

There are many things in life that we overanalyze. Many problems that we think are grand, unscalable mountains, are just clumps of dirt on an otherwise flat surface.

Most of the challenges and adversity that we face are all about perspective. The best solutions to even the most complex problems are usually the simplest.

Think of yourself as an adolescent or even a young teenager. This is an awkward time in most people's lives. Our bodies are changing, it's physically, mentally and emotionally uncomfortable.

We can feel like gargoyles, waiting for certain parts to catch up with others. Maybe you've got a huge head that your body needs to grow into. Or Dumbo ears? Huge feet?

Whatever it was for you, it's likely that you felt that you were the only one in the world, cursed to go through life looking like a freak show.

Aside from the above growing pains, everything felt like life or death. Looking back as an adult, with adult problems, those issues that seemed like life or death, where immediate, impulsive action must be taken, look trivial. It's all about perspective!

Here's the kicker, the older you get, the more experiences you get, with every notch on your belt, the problems of the past look smaller.

This is even true with "real adult problems" after a little time has passed. Ask anyone in their 60's, 70's or 80's about the problems they faced in their 30's, 40's and 50's and the answers you get might surprise you.

They are usually properly measured in response, given the specific challenge and calmly explained, using logic, how they were solved. Most of the time, if they are answering honestly, they will admit that after some level of emotional turmoil, and a bit of logic, they found a solution. They were also probably a lot of the same kinds of problems you are experiencing.

This kind of perspective used to be called wisdom. My personal definition of wisdom is this: Knowledge and perspective acquired through experience and analyzed with the proper balance of logic and emotion.

Our emotions can be a major barrier to perspective. They are usually what keep us from seeing the simplest solution.

That's why many times when you talk with someone about your problems, they hardly have to think twice about the solution. They aren't clouded with the emotional element as deeply as you are.

So, when faced with your next major obstacle, mentally take yourself out of the equation and write down the core issues. Make sure you are seeing the whole problem. Then write down the resources you have available whether they be people, money, equipment, etc.

You might have to get a little creative or think outside of the box but focus only on your resources, not the problem. If a solution doesn't immediately appear, take a break. Go for a walk, exorcise or find another way to clear your head.

Remember, the harder we look for things the harder they are to find. If you still can't think of a solution, ask someone else for their perspective. If they can't offer you an immediate solution, I bet they will give your brain that little nudge it needed to figure it out for yourself. We've all had that, "Aha" moment in situations like these.

If your obstacle is not life or death, you will either find a solution in time, realize it's not that important or the problem will solve itself (Be careful with the last option).

Ten years from now, you'll likely look back and realize how silly it was to worry as much as you did, given your new-found perspective. Or dare I say, wisdom?

The more wisdom you gain, the more fulfilling your life will be. Every rule I have laid out is purposely designed with this intention, with an opportunity for you to gain more wisdom and fulfillment.

May the sun and moon light your path to fulfillment. Let wisdom guide you in times of darkness. -JLE

SECTION 5: IN CONCLUSION

At the beginning of this book, I wrote that many of you may not find this information shocking, new or profound. That my purpose was to arrange this time-tested information together, in a way that makes it relevant to our modern lives. To give you a different perspective, with a little humor on a serious topic.

Did I make you think and question your own behaviors with honesty? Do you understand the underlying theme these 36 rules share? Do you understand why they are so important to you and to our society? Do you understand that we are not so different? Even once race, gender, culture or politics are considered? I hope so.

If much of this book seems like common sense to you, good! The simplest advice is usually the best advice and the easiest to follow.

If many of these rules are common sense to you, how many of them are you living by?

They've likely fallen out of mind as you've grown and your "problems" became priority.

Many times, we look at problems and only see bits and pieces of them. Our instinct is to focus on the parts that stand out the most. In the case of many, happiness, or lack thereof, is what stood out the most.

If the problem was a lack of happiness, all we needed to do was more of what makes us happy.

To do that, we were told that we first needed to really get to know ourselves. Turn all our focus inward. Then and only then, would we will finally figure out what makes us happy. At least that is what I've been hearing for as long as I can remember. Too bad we were trying to solve the wrong problem!

As you now know, the problem wasn't a lack of happiness, it was a lack of fulfillment. We were standing too close to the painting to see the whole image. This is yet one more case where we had the best of intentions, to only make the problem worse.

"Most of the evil in this world is done by people with good intentions" - T.S. Eliot

I wish you luck and success upon this journey. If you follow these rules, you and everyone you encounter will begin to feel more fulfilled.

If these rules catch on with others, our best days can still be ahead of us.

Fulfillment is an infectious cure, kind of like good bacteria. Even if you start with just a few of these rules, you will begin to feel more positivity in your life.

The United States is no longer bound together by similar religious ideals or a relatively homogenous culture. That is good.

Diversity of ideas, cultures, ethnicities and religions teach us many things. They bring us perspective and remember, perspective leads to wisdom.

As a warning, they can also fracture a society if we cannot embrace our similarities and share a common set of values. I believe that is the other, often unspoken challenge we face, in this modern era.

Remember, just as you could not have joy without sadness, within every benefit lays a potential challenge.

Will this list of 36 rules to fulfillment be what unites us? That common set of values that will bring us all together as one people? Values that we can share together, while still respecting our various religious beliefs, cultural practices, or sexual identities? I would love to believe it's possible. Which is why I have done my best, to define them as I have.

It must, however, start with you! Make the most of your time on this planet.

Try to do more good than harm and remember, as enchanting as it may be, don't chase happiness!

SECTION 6: ABOUT THE AUTHOR

Joshua was born in the early 1980s and grew up in the small town of Saratoga, California. He gained his knowledge through a combination of education, experience, entrepreneurship, travel, observation and parenting.

He started his career selling industrial lighting to businesses throughout the greater Los Angeles area. He learned that he had a knack for people as well as finance and then went to work as a Business Banker for a large financial institution in Palo Alto, CA.

After working in the Business to Business sector for several years, he was given an opportunity to travel to South America and become an entrepreneur.

He co-opened and managed a beachfront restaurant and bar, where he shared stories and meals with travelers from all over the world, even a few government diplomats.

The United States was his home and as enriching of an experience as this was, he sold the restaurant to return.

Business was still his passion and he immediately went to work as an Account Manager for a medical device company. He was quickly promoted to Sales Manager and Marketing Specialist.

Joshua has always wanted to reach as many people as possible, with everything he did and marketing became a way to talk to hundreds or thousands of people simultaneously, verses one by one with sales.

He was then offered a position as a Creative and Strategic Consultant for an advertising agency, which he accepted and learned a great deal from. He worked with businesses large and small, minutes away from Sand Hill Road. The venture capital center of the USA, if not the world.

His entrepreneurial spirit was still very much alive, so he later decided to open his own marketing agency. While building up his own client list, for steady income, he took another position as the in-house Marketing Manager for a national business brokerage firm.

As much as Joshua was passionate about business, an altruistic side started to emerge. He decided to return to school and become an EMT.

He found it incredibly interesting and wanted to be able to do everything he could to help people on the scene of an emergency.

That required returning to school again and completing a very intense, Paramedic program.

This enabled him to learn how to diagnose and treat life-threatening emergencies, with emergency pharmaceuticals and advanced life support techniques.

Joshua worked in Emergency Medicine for 6 years but continued marketing on the side.

He also worked as a Volunteer/Reserve Firefighter where he was promoted to Lieutenant. He loved the work he did, however, during that time, he met his wife, got married and then had a son.

California was where he was born and raised but it had grown a little too crowded for him.

He wanted his son to grow up in a smaller community, like the one that he had. They moved to Colorado where he works in Public Safety full time and continues strategic business and personal consulting on a case by case basis.

Joshua typically takes on short term consulting projects of various sizes, both personal and professional.

His talent is quickly finding the center of your current issue and providing a personalized, step by step solution. If you have an interest in exploring his services, please send an email to: **thestrategicperspective@gmail.com**.

Joshua has worked directly with some of the most powerful business people in the country as well as many doctors and lawyers, some of which are still great friends and acquaintances.

He has used strategic communication to de-escalate violent situations with murderers, rapists, and the severely mentally ill.

He has delivered babies in people's homes and officially called the time of death, for people killed in tragic accidents. He has helped save lives and consoled the families of those he could not save.

Staying true to his continued life-long desire to do everything he could, with everything he had, he has written this book to share his perspective and help others.

A humanitarian and strategic perspective unique to him alone.

SECTION 7: SOURCES

I have sourced a large amount of information from interviews with individual people, of varying walks of life, over a long period of time. As I have mentioned over and over, much of this information is not new in and of itself. Some of the information I include is directly from my experience working in health and human services. Others may be sourced from various journals, religious material or scientific studies. While others may be from my personal travels around the world.

However, everything written has been interpreted through my own unique perspective, unless speaking directly to verifiable science or a specific, named, peer reviewed study. I have listed some of the sites used in my research below. If you have additional questions on a topic, not specifically covered in my sources list, Google is your friend:

- merriam-webster.com
- technologyadvice.com
- psychologytoday.com
- health.harvard.edu
- chemistryislife.com
- positivepsychologyprogram.com
- en.wikipedia.org
- mayoclinic.org
- richarddawkins.net
- cdc.gov
- bjs.gov
- healthline.com
- gallup.com
- forbes.com

Made in the USA
Middletown, DE
18 July 2019